What clients are saying about Voge and Hugh and The Releasing Process:

"As I began to release the hindrances to my heart's desires, I began creating my heart's desires! I have increased my net worth by more than $105,000 through The Releasing Process."

—Richard Van Cleave, Mortgage Broker

"I love how The Releasing Process bypasses the mind and goes directly to your cells. I was able to transform obstacles that once stopped me. I love having this book now as a resource for those challenging times or when I get stuck."

—Nancy Cullen, Retired Businesswoman

"The course we took with Voge and Hugh transformed our relationship and our marriage! Having this book will keep us on target."

—Akash and Satyam Von Rubin, Contractor and Massage Therapist

"My house and Twin Flame partner arrived after I did this work ten years ago. I came back because I now want even more from life. The possibilities are endless this time!"

—N. Dole, Physical Therapist

"As a direct result of this work, my weight has reduced, my diabetes and blood pressure are within normal range, and I'm off my medication. How about that?! I'm feeling healthier all the time! I am so very grateful to Voge and Hugh for their ongoing support for me in my journey."

—Judi Friedman, Business Consultant

"I recently came across a workshop notebook dated 1995. I was shocked at how effective this work with Voge and Hugh Smith has been. In this Releasing Process, issues that had a deep pattern and strong effect on the quality of my life completed themselves to such an extent that I had a hard time believing that they ever existed. If it were not for the notes, there would be little proof! Blessings to you and your work."

—Cheryl Carter, Artist

Aug 22/04

I Release!

Dearest Fay
Thank-you for your endorsement
and enthusiasm for our
work...
Dearest Ronn
Thank-you for your support
and being on our team
Thank-you Both for your
friendship, trust and love!
much love
Voze

Fay + Ronn : I appreciate
your shared commitment to
truth and a healed planet.
♡ Hugh

I Release!

Create the Life That Makes Your Heart Sing

Voge and Hugh Smith

iUniverse, Inc.
New York Lincoln Shanghai

I Release!
Create the Life That Makes Your Heart Sing

iUniverse, Inc.

For information address:
iUniverse, Inc.
2021 Pine Lake Road, Suite 100
Lincoln, NE 68512
www.iuniverse.com

ISBN: 0-595-31290-X

Printed in the United States of America

Contents

ACKNOWLEDGMENTS

We want to thank the many teachers, counselors, and therapeutic and spiritual practices that have contributed to the work we do today.

We are deeply thankful for the wisdom and guidance of Osho Rajneesh, and particularly for his active meditations, which propelled so many seekers to break through their neuroses and have a glimpse of their Original Face.

To Wadud and Waduda, who taught us to see, Lisa De Long-champs, who taught us to create and the Lindwalls, who taught us to Release.

We thank all the courageous souls who have participated in our Releasing workshops over the years. It has been a joy watching you as you open more and more to the Light and love that is your birthright.

We particularly wish to express our gratitude to our gaggle of geese: Chris Hatfield, Linda Lee, Karen Ashley, Jill Scillitani, Ruth Kellogg, Mu'afrida Bell, Judi Friedman for their willingness to jump into the Releasing Laboratory each month since 1995. And thank you, Judi, for all your helpful suggestions on our first draft.

To Richard Van Cleave, our personal Releasing Ranger, who made sure that everyone he loved was touched by The Releasing Process.

With deep gratitude, we thank Elianne Obadia, our editor, the best midwife a writer could have, who with encouragement, suggestions, and thoroughness kept us on track and held us in her heart.

FOREWORD

By Dr. Isa and Yolanda Lindwall

It is a pleasure to write a foreword for this much-needed book.

In 1978, we developed The Releasing Process, and have applied it with people from all races and cultures in thirty-three countries during the past twenty-two years.

The Releasing Process can be described as a process of identifying the blocking energies that can be compared to a computer virus in cyberspace. One can then make a conscious choice to seek out the unwanted virus and release it. To some, it seems simplistic to think that a mere statement of "I release" can have such a profound impact on a person's life, but more than twenty years of experience with people from all over the world has proven to us that those who so choose can take charge of their thoughts and actions to perform so-called miracles.

It takes a brave person to undertake the responsibility of uncovering their true nature by neutralizing the false illusions and programs that stand in the way. We have found the true nature of humanity to be kind and loving once the negative imprints have been deleted from our biological computers, the human brain.

We think enough people are ready to accept the challenges that face us to make a good start. As these individuals test The Releasing Process and prove its efficacy in their own lives, the results will spread like a brilliant light, awakening the masses to their divine, unlimited nature. This book, *I Release!* indicates the potential for just such a breakthrough.

We have known Voge and her husband, Hugh, for fourteen years, having had close contact with them during many workshops. They have demonstrated consistent dedication in applying the Releasing method in their personal and professional lives. What Voge and Hugh present in this book is far more than theory; they have successfully applied it, both to themselves and others, despite obstacles that would have defeated those with less persistence.

Their manuscript contains a sincerity that comes from an inner knowing that can only be gained from personal experience. We invite you to join their ranks as you read this book and discover its value in your own life.

We highly recommend *I Release!* It is written in an easy, flowing style that brings great clarity to the process. We encourage everyone who feels drawn to this subject to read this book thoroughly and put The Releasing Process to the test. The life you change will be your own.

AUTHORS' PREFACE

Individually and collectively, we are participating in a spiritual awakening on our planet. More and more people are finally realizing that much of their pain, be it physical or emotional, actually originates on a deeper, soul level, and that until it gets dealt with at that level, the pain will continue. An unwillingness to consider personal issues and pain within a spiritual context means that we are missing a profound opportunity for personal growth and transformation.

The Releasing Process is a therapeutic process that can help you discover your role in this awakening, while assisting you on your path toward wholeness.

We want to show you that there is no pain in your life that cannot be relieved, no incident in your life from which you were never meant to heal, no heartache so great you cannot be free of its grip, no lack that cannot be replaced by unlimited abundance, and no emptiness so deep that it cannot be filled with Divine Love.

This is our purpose, this is your purpose, and this is where we meet.

I Release! is designed as a workbook to take you on a powerful journey from being a seeker to a finder. Whatever your focus is—your body, career and relationships, or your purpose and spiritual fulfillment—*I Release!* shows how you can move from point A to point B in fulfilling your heart's desires.

This great tale by Rabindrinath Tagore, a Hindu poet and mystic beautifully illustrates the confusion many of us experience as seekers on the Path:

"I was searching for God for thousands of lives. I saw him...sometimes far away...I rushed...but by the time I would reach there he had gone further. It went on and on. But finally I arrived at a door, and on the door was a sign: "This is the house where God lives."

For the first time I became worried. I became very troubled. Trembling, I went up the stairs. I was just going to knock on the door when suddenly, in a flash, I saw...If I knock on the door and God opens the door, then what? Then everything is finished! My journeys, my pilgrimages, my great adventures, my philosophy, my poetry, all the longing in my heart—all is finished! It will be a suicide! So I removed my shoes from my feet...because going back down the stairs might create some noise...And from the moment I reached the bottom of the steps, I ran. And I have not looked back. Since then I have been running and running for thousands of years.

Of course I am still searching for God, but now I know where he lives. So all I have to do is avoid that house...that house haunts me. I remember it perfectly. If by chance I accidentally enter that house, then all is finished."

I Release! is our invitation to you: Postpone no longer. Open the door, step through, and allow yourself to have what you've been seeking all this time.

It has been our dream to write this book to share the powerful healing that can occur through this new therapy, The Releasing Process. Although this book is written in Voge's voice, the two of us have created it together and it reflects both of our experiences and passion about our work. It is our prayer that this book will help you achieve *your* dreams.

With love and appreciation,
Voge and Hugh

INTRODUCTION

For many years, throughout our twenties and thirties, Hugh and I focused on our own inner paths toward wholeness, trusting that a time would come when we would be ready to share our gifts with the world.

By 1991, we had been offering workshops, private sessions, and couple counseling for many years. We had accumulated a wealth of therapeutic training and experience over the previous decade and, combining that with my clairvoyant gifts and our love for the work, we were doing our best to serve the needs of our clients. However, we were still searching for a way to work with clients that would incorporate the spiritual dimension (an important part of our lives) into our emphasis on experiential forms of therapy.

In the spring of 1991, we had the pleasure of meeting Dr. Isa Lindwall and his wife, Yolanda, when a mutual friend organized a weekend workshop for them in the San Francisco Bay Area. We participated in that workshop, and after experiencing the depth and effectiveness of The Releasing Process, we knew we had found the missing piece for our work. That weekend was also a training in the use of The Releasing Process, and we immediately incorporated this powerful, spiritually based technique into our work with clients. It was a perfect fit. With Releasing, we were able to zero in on the root cause of our clients' problems and, as with all true healing, a spiritual component permeated the process.

Two years later, we took a week-long training with Isa and Yolanda in Arkansas. Prior to the training, I had been offering psychic readings and was becoming frustrated and dissatisfied, recognizing that predict-

ing someone's future didn't truly serve or empower them. Upon returning home, I began to use my clairvoyant abilities in a new and more
powerful way. I had prayed for Spirit to show me new ways to use my
clairvoyance that would lead to true transformation in my life and my
clients' lives. The melding of The Releasing Process with my clairvoyance was the answer to these prayers.

Now, instead of telling a person when their true love was going to
show up, I was able to help them release the inner programs and bankrupt beliefs I saw inside them that compelled them to attract the wrong
people. Another typical scenario was a client asking if they were going
to make his or her fortune with the latest marketing scheme. Instead of
answering them, I had them release whatever was inside them that
could actually repel the success their heart desired.

You see, it doesn't matter if your beloved shows up, or your financial
ship comes in, if inside of you, you don't feel worthy of receiving. You
will continue to push away all blessings that come into your life.

As this new phase of our work deepened, I found myself accessing
not only the clients' memories, but also the damaging effects those
memories had on their lives. I even saw the debilitating effects in their
organs, muscle tissue and spine.

Many clients were delighted and relieved to receive these insights.
They experienced profound healing in their lives, from the physical
upward to the spiritual. However, others were uncomfortable and
unwilling to embrace this information. Many people live in resignation,
not realizing that they've painted themselves into a corner and are no
longer open to the potential for miracles, joy and fulfillment in their
lives. Those souls, and the ones who only wanted a "psychic hotline"
session and were unwilling to feel the pain of their own mis-creations,
stopped coming.

A new quality of client is required for this work: individuals who are
courageous and honest with themselves, willing to dive deeply into their
healing process. It requires that they be ready to let go of masks and
pretenses, to fully experience their naked vulnerability. We understand

that this is a tall order, and yet it is the only way toward wholeness and genuine peace.

I

The Releasing Process

Each time one of us achieves mastery over our physical reality; we expand the highway of light into the octaves of perfection, creating a wider passage for the rest of humanity. That is our most important service at this time.

—Patricia Cota-Robles

1

How to Read and Use
I Release!

Throughout the book, you will read stories of how people's lives have been transformed through The Releasing Process, and we hope you find these to be interesting and even inspirational. However, you also have the opportunity to actually experience how The Releasing Process can work for you.

The processes taught in this book are easy to grasp, and they work.

Following a couple of important requirements on your part will maximize the benefit you will receive.

This is a workbook. It requires you to actually do the exercises for any results to occur. It is essential to appreciate the difference between understanding a concept with your mind and having an experience from your Being.

To illustrate this, we want to tell you about a client who took our *Two Wings to God* workshop several years ago. He was very earnest and went to great lengths to explain his commitment to leading a spiritual life. During a guided meditation, he went back to his childhood and relived an experience of a church service he had attended. He had been so moved by the singing of the choir that he began to cry. Embarrassed adults ushered him outside because of this inappropriate behavior. After the exercise, with tears in his eyes, he whispered, "It was God. I felt

God through their singing. All this time, I thought I knew God, but it was just a concept in my mind." Since then, he reclaimed that part of himself that could allow an experience of God, instead of merely having knowledge about a concept of God.

Do not distance yourself from having an experience, merely reading to accumulate more knowledge or information; you will miss an opportunity for true growth. If you read the exercises and engage only your mind, you might hear yourself thinking, "Why are they making me do this? It doesn't make any sense." Or you might think, "I know why they are having me do this. I won't bother doing the exercise because I already know the outcome."

The Releasing Process is not about drawing conclusions or adding to your knowledge. The exercises are designed to elicit memories, feelings, and reactions, bringing to the surface your awareness of whatever needs to be released. A willingness to risk and even be a little foolish is encouraged.

The book is divided into two parts:

Part One, The Releasing Process is explanatory, and includes:

- How to use The Workbook

- How The Releasing Process works

- The significance of memory and emotions

Part Two, The Workbook, is experiential.
You will have a personal experience of releasing through addressing The Ten Hindrances to Your Heart's Desires.

This is a threefold process:

- Identify the heart's desire

- Face the memories, fears, and feelings that hinder your heart's desire

- Release the hindrance, clearing any resistance so you can have your heart's desire

When you read The Ten Hindrances, you will resonate with some more strongly than others. Work initially with the ones that elicit the strongest reaction.

We offer three different ways to work:

1. Guided meditations

2. Exercises

3. The hallmark of our work, The Releasing Process itself

The Releasing Process is also illustrated for you through the stories of many of our clients through the years. You are encouraged to reflect on what needs to be released for yourself if you find you relate to the stories being told. You can repeat others' releasing statements for yourself, alter their statements to fit your situation, or create new ones. Soon you will become proficient in discovering what else you need to release.

During our seminars, we encourage participants to repeat to themselves the releasing statements of the person on whom we are focused. There is a universal quality to virtually all the problems we face in life, and when we open our heart, we feel a camaraderie and parallel movement in growth with others. Over and over, it has happened that while working with one person in a group, we notice that three others are crying because they're releasing the same things for themselves. Often, they will thank the person we were working with for bringing it to the surface for them to heal. Elisabeth Kubler-Ross once said, "We are all on death row." In a similar way, we are all participants in this group therapy we call life.

We suggest that you do fifteen minutes of Releasing every day as part of your practice. It is a great way to get squeaky clean from the residue of your past. I will be starting you out with examples of what I've released in myself and others.

In our workshops and private sessions, there's a verbal exchange in which our clients repeat the releasing statements we give them. However, when you put the statements in writing, it can be just as dynamic, if not more so. In fact, it's the way we do releasing for ourselves. The key to effective releasing statements is simply a sincerity and willingness to allow the emotions to surface. No expertise or training is required. We have witnessed many lives transformed in an instant from a single powerful releasing statement. It only takes one. And if you create one each day, you will find yourself moving into a very potent space of integrity and wholeness. Out of that wholeness, you may create your heart's desires. And isn't that what we are all here to do?

2

The Releasing Process
and How It Works

How could one simple releasing statement create such change?

While growing up in the Bronx, I was often told by my mother, "Voge you're too much!" "Ma, can I have that box? I want to open up a lemonade stand with Ellen Murphy up on Castle Hill Ave."

"You're five years old and you want to sell lemonade to strangers? You're too much!" "Ma, can I have money to buy some crepe paper? I've just organized all the kids on the block and we're going to put on a show!"

"You've done what? You're too much!"

"Ma, I'm going to this great concert; I'll be gone for three days to a town in upstate New York called Woodstock."

"You're too much!"

As I grew up, others joined my mother's chorus, reminding me of my too much-ness. The nuns who taught me, boys I dated, and well-meaning girlfriends constantly reminded me that I was dangerously close to going outside the lines of what was considered normal and appropriate. It was always said in a way to shame, rather than to encourage.

In my thirties, I met and fell in love with Hugh. The topic of living together came up in conversation, and I said something to him that was somewhere between a gentle hint and getting in his face. He looked me right in the eyes and said, "Voge, you're too much!" The words I had come to dread had just come out of my beloved's mouth. I was taken aback. Should I defend, back down, explain, or walk away? What he said next took me totally by surprise: "And, I love your too-muchness!"

What did he say?

I was too much, and he loved me for it! I never knew how much I had longed to hear those words until he spoke them.

That one simple little statement released a lifetime of shame, freed my soul and made it soar!

That sentence changed my life. Since that day, I have claimed my too-muchness, and no one has told me that I am too much in a way that shamed me. Or if they tried, I never noticed because a radical, internal shift of my energy had taken place and I was virtually a new person.

It is this quality of experience that allows one simple releasing statement to create profound change and transformation in an individual. Many of our new clients are skeptical that a releasing statement can have so much power until they get in touch with an important early childhood decision and feel how much power *that* decision had in altering their entire life.

As we all learned in high school physics, we aren't actually solid matter, we are made up of energy. This life energy (known in other traditions as *chi* or *prana*) flows through us constantly. But as the years go by and we collect experiences, we tend to redirect this flow into our memory banks, where it solidifies into cellular knowledge, decisions we make about the way life is. Each moment of our experience is filtered through this baggage of acquired knowledge, so instead of responding authentically in the present moment with the full force of our life energy, we react on the basis of past experiences and decisions we've made about life and, even more significantly, about ourselves. In fact, all negative emotions originate in these hidden memory banks so much so that what you think you're upset about is rarely what you're truly upset about. Usually a button that's pressed in the present activates programming from your past, setting off the old alarms and fears.

The goal is to become neutral, that is, free of our programming from the past that restricts us from living in our natural state of joyful deservedness. The more neutral we are about our past, the more we can allow in the blessings that the universe continuously showers on us in the present. Therein lies the value and power of The Releasing Process. It not only brings you an awareness of how you've been organizing yourself based on the past, but it dismantles the rigid cellular knowledge you've held in place, which torments you by insisting, "You can't have that. These limitations are real, so get used to it!"

Take a moment now and consider the ramifications of this. See how profoundly your life is affected by having your life energy and all the cells of your Being filtered through your past fears, traumas, and limiting beliefs. It is this scenario that The Releasing Process addresses so effectively.

I had a powerful introduction to The Releasing Process in a session with "Doc" Isa Lindwall, who, with his wife Yolanda, originated the process. By speaking aloud to me a series of statements, he had me release the shock that I still held in the cells of my physical body from losing my leg at the age of nine. Not only could I feel the shock leaving my body; what also left was the constricted way I had learned to hold myself physically, emotionally, and energetically to retain the shock. The next moment, I felt my spine realign itself. Each releasing statement he spoke informed me of the way I'd been organizing and controlling my energy. Simultaneously, block by block, the internal structures I'd created to hold myself together after that one traumatic experience were dismantling.

How could one simple releasing statement create such change?

There's an old expression, "The blood remembers what the mind forgets," and the noted medical intuitive Carolyn Myss has said, "Your biography creates your biology."

These are both ways of saying that so much of our experience, no matter how long ago even lifetimes ago—is still encoded in our Being.

And whether a traumatic or painful experience is stored in your blood, DNA, astral body, emotional body, chakras, or physical body, The Releasing Process intuitively goes to this encoding and brings it to your awareness, thereby setting you free of its influence.

Just as your physical body has ways of releasing toxins, so does your energetic body. During a Releasing session, you may declare from your Being, "I release the pain in my heart from feeling that my Light was not recognized when I came into the physical body." As you speak that out loud, your throat chakra acts as the sanitation department of your energetic body and releases the pain toxins in which you have been marinating. Unfortunately, a description of the mere mechanics falls short of capturing the richness of the experience, but when you apply the process, you taste the results.

The Releasing Process transforms lives through a powerful convergence of memory, emotion, and commitment to your Truth.

It was mentioned earlier that our natural state is one of deservedness and joy. One of the hardest things to face is how we deny ourselves this joy and stop ourselves from having what would make our heart sing. Although many of us believe we are the creators of our reality, when actually confronted with some of our creations, we retreat into blame, victimhood and guilt. These are the reactions of one who is spiritually immature. An acknowledgment of our responsibility, coupled with a desire to learn from our mis-creations and change, demonstrates spiritual maturity.

Even one releasing statement can create tremendous change in one's life. Releasing is experiential, and as you let go of your past mis-creations, you clearly see and feel the direct impact they've had on your life. You see the choices you made to create the mess you're in, and your responsibility is inescapable. All of our clients find this empowering and liberating.

There is nothing worse than the helpless feeling of not being able to see the reason or cause for something in our life. When an expert suggests that the root of our problem exists at some causative level we can't see—whether it's the unconscious, subconscious, past lives, or the astral plane—it can be frightening and frustrating. We may fear, "If the cause is below my level of awareness, how can I take on the task of bringing it up to my awareness?"

The Releasing Process accesses that source not through analysis or knowledge but through one's Being, with assistance from Spirit. This book will help you face some of your creations and develop your inner sight so that the things you were once blind to can now be brought to the light of day to be purified and released.

3

The Power of Memories

Many times each week memory makes me a child again.

—Wally Lamb, *She's Come Undone*

Memories are among the most pervasive and powerful forces in human consciousness. They cling to the psyche of our soul with the potential to wreak havoc or create bliss in our present state of being. It all depends on the decisions we have made about each memory. We all have neutral memories, positively charged memories, and negatively charged memories.

When I'm shopping and walk past the make-up counter, there's a certain smell of vanilla that connects me to my Aunt Dolly; I remember how her fragrance could fill a room. It catches me by surprise and I turn around, half expecting to see her there at the end of the aisle. Then I'm reminded of when I was a little girl in the hospital after losing my leg in a car accident—how Aunt Dolly would douse me with this magic scent from a little bottle she carried in her large patent leather pocket-book—and I feel the love and compassion she had for me during a difficult time.

There's a certain way the smell of sea salt can hit my nose on a windy day and I'm right back on the pier of the D.A. Beach Club we went to when I was a child living in the Bronx. When I go out to get the mail in the afternoon, I'll brush by the flowers of the hedge outside our home, and their fragrance smells like jelly beans to me. When I get a good whiff, I'm back in our Gleason Avenue apartment on Easter morning, joyfully opening my bunny basket filled with candy.

From the moment we start breathing, we begin to collect the memories that frame us and inform us of who we think we are and what we believe to be true about life. I've shared some fairly neutral memories from my childhood, which nonetheless convey the pervasiveness of memory.

Perhaps while reading this, you too can feel a memory lodged in your heart that transports you back to your childhood.

You might notice that, along with the neutral memories, you access a charged memory from which you have formed a strong decision or belief. For example, you may have a memory from your childhood that makes you feel separate from a family member—a memory that isolates you, even shuts down your vitality and life energy. You may have learned to reopen that part of your heart to the person associated with the memory, but a childhood decision that you made at the time of the incident may still be exerting its influence in your adult life. Perhaps something like, "When I open up my heart, I get hurt."

This thought or belief may not even be conscious, but it is still lurking inside, waiting to warn you. A similar experience may then happen in your life, and you automatically close your heart, unwilling to risk it being broken again.

And yet we will insist that we've done this because "I know this person isn't trustworthy." Or "I'm not going to risk being made a fool again." There can be any number of other rationalizations to justify your position. But it's crucial to notice that your original decision was born out of a painful memory, and its sole job is to remind you, "Be careful! Keep your heart closed and protect yourself from this kind of experience again." And you wall off yet another piece of your heart. Is any of this sounding familiar?

And so we become adults, which for most of us means acting world-weary, sophisticated, serious, cynical, and predictable. What a miraculous thing it would be if we could regain that boundless energy, trust and enthusiasm for life that we took for granted as a child! The American Heritage Dictionary defines enthusiasm as, "ecstasy arising from the possession by God."

This state of Being truly is our birthright. It is available to us when we have the courage to be fully alive and present in the here and now. Clinging to our self-limiting beliefs and paralyzing fears from our past ensures that we will live out our days as jaded adults.

C.G. Jung comments on this in his autobiography, *Memories, Dreams and Reflections*:

> *I have frequently seen people become neurotic when they content themselves with inadequate or wrong answers to the questions of life. They seek position, marriage, reputation, outward success or money, and remain unhappy even when they have attained what they were seeking. Such people are usually confined within too narrow a Spiritual horizon. Their life has not sufficient meaning. If they are able to develop into more spacious personalities, their neurosis generally disappears.*

I witness the profound effects of memory each time I do a session with a client, beginning with counting them down into a relaxed state to delve into their past. I pray, "Spirit Most High, we ask you to awaken whatever memory most needs to be healed at this time." And I watch as it comes bubbling to the surface, with all its detail, drama, and significance. The power that the memory exerts over the client, and which often dominates their current life, becomes obvious to them because they become fully involved with the inner images and impressions from their past.

I then may ask them, "How is what you experienced in the past similar to what is going on in your life now?" Relief floods through them as they begin to connect the dots linking the decisions and beliefs based on the memories to the current situations and patterns that are plaguing them. They make the essential shift from the world of effect, in which they are a victim, to the world of cause, where they are the creator and can enjoy the resulting sense of freedom.

We then move into the actual Releasing part of the process to let go of the heaviness and negativity of these bankrupt beliefs and obsolete childhood decisions. A new lightness and energy is felt as all the client's mis-creations based on these memories are transformed into a healthier and more positive way of perceiving their life.

Avoiding painful memories has become a full-time job for many people. Inviting up old nightmares is the last thing in the world they would choose. Not everyone has the intelligence and courage to initiate this healing process. I would compare it to the pain felt during a deep massage. Initially, you may recoil as the masseur digs into your shoulder, but as you learn to allow it, breathing deeply through the temporary discomfort, you come to know it's a "good hurt" and that you will feel so much more relaxed and at home in your body afterward. Similarly, when we consciously choose to feel those old emotional hurts we've been carrying for years, they become a healthy growing pain; no matter how acute they feel at first. We become free of bitterness, tension, and anxiety. We then understand that:

If we close our heart to suffering, we cannot open it to love.

To illustrate the process I've just described, I will share some actual sessions with several clients.

I must stress that our sessions and workshops are conducted in an atmosphere of love, respect, and trust. We are intimately familiar with the emotionally vulnerable states that result from this work, because we have delved into these realms in our own journey toward health and wholeness. Once again we defer to C.G. Jung who wrote, "Only the wounded physician heals."

Alice and Jerry

Alice was having trouble in her marriage. After seeing me for a few sessions, she sent her husband. Jerry didn't believe that anything from his past could be affecting him in the present, much less have anything to do with the problems in his marriage. He was very stoic. When I counted him down, he kept saying, "I don't see anything." After twenty minutes of nothing happening, I tried a few things to get his energy going and then asked him, "Are you still not seeing anything?" He replied, "Well, from the moment you started to count me down, I kept seeing the tree in my backyard from when I was a little boy—but what's that got to do with anything?"

I encouraged him to trust what his subconscious was sending him and imagine that he was that little boy looking up at the tree. He immediately started trembling, and I could see a tremendous amount of emotion coming to the surface. I asked what he was seeing. Tears ran down his face as he said, "My mother would take a switch from that tree and beat me with it." Slowly, we began connecting the dots as we accessed the decisions, beliefs, and attitudes that were formed from this brutality. Jerry also said, "I had forgotten about those beatings and how they made me feel. She told me that if I cried, I would get more of the same."

Hearing this, I remembered Alice saying that Jerry's mother seemed to have some kind of power over him, even dictating the religion of her grandchildren. Alice would plead with Jerry to keep his mother out of their relationship, but he would argue that Alice should be more understanding because his mother was a widow and they were now her only family.

Jerry was shocked to see that a hidden memory was dominating his life in present time. This was not some New Age belief but a gut-level experience in which he saw how he'd relinquished his power to his mother during those beatings. He felt how her verbal attacks caused a part of his spirit to break off. He also recognized how he had remained at the effect of his mother and that it was destroying his marriage. As The Releasing Process unfolded, it was incredibly moving to see him integrating the part of his spirit that had broken off during the beatings. He went from sobbing to laughing as he reclaimed his innocence, playfulness, and joy.

I saw Alice a week later. "Thank you, thank you," was all she could manage through her tears at first. And then: "I was about to give up on him, but Jerry came home a different man!" Several times that week, Jerry stood up to his mother, something he had never done because he wanted to keep the peace. Within the year, Jerry and Alice moved to Connecticut, where they'd always wanted to live but hadn't because of Jerry's mother. More than eight years later, we still receive updates on how well they are doing.

Alice and Jerry were finally able to create a partnership of mature love that is possible only when the old, unconscious, and unfulfilled needs are brought into the light of day—and released.

From the moment we are born, and even as early as the inception of our soul, we begin to collect memories on which deeply felt decisions are based, beliefs formed, attitudes built, and vows are made. Using the computer as a metaphor, the aforementioned comprise the programs that go into the hard drive of our soul. These programs from our past shape our personalities, our psychology, and our biology, and even pre-determine our future.

Consequently, we build our future not from the rich fullness of the here and now but from the memories, fears, and out-of-date programs of our past. In fact, we allow these programs to determine crucial life choices for us: the amount of self-love we give ourselves, the quality of partners and relationships we allow, the types of jobs and income we create, and the goals and vision, to which we aspire. Our programming even imprints a predisposition toward specific diseases.

So to say these that programs limit the potential of all that we could be is an understatement. To ponder the effects all of this has on one's life is to understand how most of us remain separate from our heart's desires. We stubbornly insist on the limitations prescribed by our programs while saying, ironically, to anyone who will listen: "This is just the way life is."

Sadly, we are so convinced that the programs we created are reality that we've forgotten who we truly are: innocent and beautiful expressions of the Divine, free to express the full potential of our unique selves whenever we choose. Referring to this state of affairs, an enlightened teacher from Russia named George I. Gurdjieff said simply:

Until you become horrified at yourself, you have not begun to truly know yourself.

Melissa

Melissa attended one of our *Money is Just the Metaphor* workshops. She couldn't understand why she was always in debt and had been for her entire adult life. She cried in the group as she explained that no matter how much she cut back on her lifestyle, disciplining herself to pay off her credit cards, she'd find herself back in debt within a year—most recently for fifteen thousand dollars.

She was desperate to get to the bottom of this. When we worked with her, she accessed a memory from her childhood, in which she heard her mother constantly saying, "You're going to have to pay for being here." When Melissa came out of that memory, all she could say was, "And I've been paying ever since!" One little statement repeated over and over by her mother, the person she believed in the most, established the pattern and program that defined Melissa's life. No amount of financial counseling or budgeting can overcome the power of a childhood vow, which for Melissa became a vow of poverty. A new peace of mind came to Melissa when she discovered the memory that was at the core of her feeling powerless. She also had an awareness of the truth that would now set her free from this seemingly irreversible situation.

Joanne

In one of our workshops, Joanne shared her frustration at being fifty-five years old and still house-sitting or sleeping on friend's couches. She longed for her own home. When we worked with her, she relived an experience from when she was in her mother's womb. Joanne was conceived by a sixteen-year-old girl from a very poor family and was given up for adoption a week after she was born. In her session, she felt the anxiety of being in the womb of this young girl who was in so much conflict. The energetic transmission broadcasting so strongly from her mother was, "There's not enough money for a home for this baby." Powerful programming for a baby to feel! When Joanne opened her eyes, she said to us, "I've been looking for that piece my whole life. It explains so much. There were times I was just about to rent a place, and then some emergency would pop up and the money would have to go to that instead. It all makes sense to me now." We will return to Joanne's story later in the book.

Everyone who walks through the door of my office or participates in our workshops wants something. Jerry and Alice wanted to save their marriage. Melissa wanted to be debt-free. Joanne wanted a home. The Releasing Process is universal in that it addresses any person's unique situation. Within the process itself is an intrinsic wisdom that focuses our attention on the underlying root cause of the problem. This goes much deeper than the mind's understanding which would never see a connection between a failing marriage and a tree, a daughter's debt to her mother's badgering, and a homeless woman's quest to a fear released in her mother's womb.

The key to living a fulfilled life in the present is found in our past. The Releasing Process is one of the simplest and most effective formats for mining your memories and unlocking valuable insights and "aha!"s to get your life back on track.

4

Emotions: The Key to Healing

The following is a list of common myths and beliefs that actually retard our growth. See if you identify with any of them:

- There are good emotions and bad emotions.

- I shouldn't be feeling (sad, angry, happy, etc.)

- Emotions make me weak and vulnerable.

- If I am spiritual, then I should be beyond my emotions.

- If I feel too much, it might overwhelm me and I'll go crazy.

- I'm never going to let (her, him) see my emotions.

- I'm just not the emotional type.

- If I understand the situation, I won't need to show my emotions.

I remember a story about John F. Kennedy, Jr. During a skiing trip with the Kennedy clan, when he was a teenager, he fell and hurt himself and began to cry. One of his cousins went over to him and said, "Kennedys don't cry." John's reply was simply, "Not this Kennedy!"

Most of us were raised to be good Kennedys who don't cry when we are hurt. A healthy expression of the full rainbow of human emotions is not encouraged in our society. Emotions are seen as flaws that must be eliminated in a neurotic pursuit of perfection. Of course, the repression of these imperfections further distorts and magnifies them. This, in turn, feeds our fear of those repressed emotions, which slowly take on the form of a monster in the closet.

It becomes even more complicated when we add our rationalizations and justifications for not expressing our sadness, anger, and joy. For example, we'll convince ourselves that our closets are clean as long as we keep the door closed, but meanwhile we're perpetuating the process of numbing ourselves to those "bad" or "scary" emotions.

We exact a high price for keeping that door closed. Feminist author Germaine Greer tells a story about one aspect of this phenomenon:

> *I was giving prizes to a class that had just graduated from high school and up came all these girls with double-A grades and their little Ally McBeal sparrow hands and little sparrow legs. They're my best students and high achievers and completely anorexic. Then another bunch of girls came up, and they were enormous. They came up clumping, walking with their feet apart and making a big play out of being clumsy and stupid. The two are opposite sides of the same coin; both are apologizing for themselves. What I didn't see was a girl who was just healthy, strong and confident. And it's not just to do with boys or fashion. It's got a lot more to do with being full of anger and hostility and having no way of expressing it.*

The numbing of emotions has caused an epidemic of depression in our culture. And as the above example indicates, depression is not a cause but a symptom of much deeper emotional problems such as repressed anger and dysfunction in the family unit. The easy way out is to prescribe a drug, as if the depression could be healed in this way. In fact, this is usually only a holding pattern, a postponement of looking into the true source of one's pain. Mood-altering prescription drugs are becoming so popular and pervasive that dozens of them are now advertised on TV as remedies for depression and anxiety. Some people of course benefit from these drugs, but in general, there is no encouragement or support from psychiatry and the American Medical Association for a patient to actually experience those underlying feelings and learn what they are trying to say.

Depression is often suppressed anger redirected at ourselves. It continues to fester inside while we are being tranquilized by the drugs. The drugs have no effect whatsoever on healing the suppressed emotions. When the individual finally faces the deeper problem and integrates the accompanying emotions, the need for drugs is eliminated.

Since this book is intended for people on a spiritual journey, we also want to consider how emotions are handled in that context. What we have observed is that most spiritual seekers carry religious programming and beliefs from their childhood—and even from past lives—that insists, "If I'm spiritual, I've transcended my emotions." Looking beneath this, we see an actual longing to rise above the messiness and perceived ugliness of our feelings, especially if as a child we endured frightening emotions in the home. In our attempt to avoid their unpleasantness, we may convince ourselves that we've succeeded in actually eliminating them from our lives. Even meditation practices, such as the repeated humming of a mantra, can be employed to achieve this goal. After many years of using meditation in this manner, we become at best, peacefully neurotic.

Having invested so much time and energy in spiritual practice, people may find it difficult to take an honest look at themselves and to acknowledge that their emotions haven't been transcended, only suppressed. Laughter, sorrow, anger, and joy are healthy and integral elements on the way to the true mastery of our being. Vipassana teacher Jack Kornfield illustrates this point with the following story from his book *A Path with Heart:*

> *At one meditation retreat, I encountered a man whose only child, a four-year-old girl, had died in an accident just a few months before. Because she died in a car he was driving, he was filled with guilt as well as grief. He had stopped working and turned to full-time spiritual practice for solace. When he came to this retreat, he had already been to other retreats, he had been blessed by a great swami, and he had taken vows with a holy nun from South India. At the retreat his meditation cushion looked like a nest. It was surrounded by crystals, feathers, rosaries and pictures of various great gurus. Each time he sat he would pray to each of the gurus and*

chant and recite sacred mantras. All of this to heal himself, he said. But perhaps all of this was to ward off his grief. After a few days I asked him if he would be willing to simply sit, without all his sacred objects, without prayer or chanting or any other practice. The next time he came in he just sat. In five minutes he was crying. In ten minutes he was sobbing and wailing. He had finally let himself take the seat in the midst of his sorrow; he had finally, truly begun to grieve.

When we encounter serious seekers divorced from their feelings, we often suggest, "Instead of always trying to be more spiritual, allow yourself to be more authentic." Authenticity leads to self-acceptance and self-love—true indicators that you're on the right path.

If you are medicating, meditating, or intellectualizing as a way to avoid what you are feeling, you are missing a necessary part of your spiritual development. In fact, you need to start seeing your emotions not as hindrances but as valuable allies in facing the deepest truths about yourself.

Although it was somewhat simplistic, the book *The Celestine Prophecy* conveyed a profound truth about the spiritual journey. An aspirant's vibrational frequency begins to rise as he or she progresses. Gradually, we lose interest in the coarser aspects of our previous lifestyle. For example, we may move away from the heavier, meat and potatoes diet to lighter fare. We may drift away from negative acquaintances that tended to bring us down. In short, we burn many bridges when we sincerely search for our personal Truth.

Similarly, we can no longer hold on to the old heaviness and density in our emotional body if we want to move toward a lighter and more genuine inner peace. The anger, sadness, self-pity, and despair must be released. This is an important part of our spiritual growth.

It is something we must do consciously, by feeling. After these emotions have departed, you will feel lighter, more free and expanded. This is the purifying process of Releasing. Through our memories, we are accessing our emotional body where the charge resides. From there, the charged emotions are neutralized.

As children, we often stifled our emotions because there was neither a safe place nor permission for them. This is a regrettable yet under-standable fact of life. But if as adults we are still stifling our emotions, we'll never be completely integrated and achieve our full potential. One of the side benefits of The Releasing Process is the opportunity to reclaim the part of ourselves that broke away in childhood. The enthu-siasm and spontaneity of our youth returns once again through the syn-ergy of memory and emotion that happens during a Releasing session. This is what we believe is meant by, "Until you become as a little child, you will not enter the kingdom of heaven." What we perhaps can finally embrace is the possibility that this "kingdom of heaven" is available to us right here and right now—if we summon the courage to claim it.

Samantha

Samantha had been on a spiritual path for a long time when she first attended one of our seminars. She had adhered to a daily meditation practice for many years and yet was unable, or rather, unwilling, to feel her emotions. People could be wailing all around her, but she would sit like a spiritual warrior—untouched and unmoved, with an air of detachment about her. When talking with her about her issues, if she got dangerously close to feeling anything, she would desperately scram-ble into her mind to try to understand her emotions intellectually.

But the intellect had also been her salvation. As her story unfolded, we discovered that she had learned to retreat into her mind as a little girl when her mother died. She wasn't allowed to fully feel that loss and had essentially lived in her head ever since—terrified to feel anything below her neck. It was sad to watch her in a roomful of people who were learning to express and embrace the full gamut of their emotions. It was like watching a child in the playground who hadn't learned how to play like the other kids. The seriousness in her demeanor was so strong that the rare times she would let herself laugh came as a shock to us all.

Although Samantha's situation is extreme, it has a universal quality to which many of us can relate. Perhaps while reflecting on her story, your own memories may be reactivating some old, persistent feelings.

What follows are a few Releasing statements that addressed Samantha's plight and moved her to a lighter, more empowered way of being. We encourage you to read them aloud, and if you identify with any of them, simply allow your feelings to be stirred and see where they take you. Give yourself permission to feel—without censoring, suppressing or intellectualizing. Perhaps you might even create your own Releasing statements. And know that your spirit guides and Higher Self are with you now and always, supporting you with their love.

- I release the decision I made when my mother died that my being emotional helped cause her death.

- I release the decision I made to hide my emotions from then on.

- I release the vow I made to myself to never let anyone know what I was feeling.

- I release my fear of my feelings being used against me.

- I release the pain in my heart from my childhood, when all those confusing emotions welled up inside me.

- I release the pain of feeling isolated and abandoned when I expressed my feelings.

- I release the decision I made that emotions keep me alone.

- I release my anger and rage that there was never a listening for my emotions.

- I release my guilt and shame for feeling anger.

- I release the fear that comes up in me now as an adult when I feel emotions, believing that I have to do away with them quickly so I won't be alone.

- I release my pride in being emotionally self-sufficient.

- I release my belief that emotions make me look weak.

- I release convincing myself that not having emotions makes me powerful.

- I release my belief that emotional detachment is an indication of spiritual development.

- I release my fear of going crazy if I allow all my repressed emotions to surface.

- I release always listening to my head, and ignoring my heart.

Feel free to continue with more of your own statements until the emotional charge is gone and you feel neutral.

5

The Invitation: Toward Wholeness and Creating Your Heart's Desires

I've always been the kind of person who gets to the bottom of things. Hugh calls me a terrier with a rat. It's that kind of tenacity in my own self-inquiry that I bring to my work with clients and students.

I'm interested in the bottom line, and the bottom line I've always been interested in is the duality that exists between my saying I want something and my inability to actually create that thing in my life. Very early on, I was exasperated to find that just wanting something didn't necessarily mean I would get it. Why not?

Like many of you, I'd read manifesting books and attended workshops that taught techniques intended to help me create my heart's desires. Fueled by sheer mindforce, I'd sometimes have a glimmer of the success I sought, but invariably, it would only give me a taste and I would again collapse into my frustration. But I was determined to understand why results were so sporadic, and inconsistent. It wasn't until I experienced The Releasing Process that I discovered the absolute bottom line to success in creating my heart's desires:

To become my best, I must first face my worst!

I learned that manifesting techniques don't work because they overlook a huge part of our consciousness: the part inside of us that is lying in the fetal position underneath the sink, afraid to be successful.

Manifesting techniques and strategies deal only with the world of *effects* while The Releasing Process focuses on the world of *cause*. Techniques superimpose a kind of false yes over your hidden no and your resistance—resistance to your heart's desires, your Light, even the God within you. As long as this hidden inner resistance is ignored, you remain divided against yourself—split. Creating your heart's desires becomes a battle between these two aspects of yourself. It's no wonder that results are inconsistent. When you do have success, it is only because one aspect won a round over the other, but you are always faced with the uncertainty of who will win the next round.

By ignoring or denying this inner conflict, we continue to give power and permission to this relentless tug-of-war between our yes and our no. Having the courage to face what lies behind that no is a turning point, and it is critical to our evolution.

For years, I insisted to myself and others that I was ready and willing to meet my mate, my beloved. But I continued to fall in love with the wrong men—and blame them. Finally, in my mid-thirties and exasperated after my latest failed fling, I turned to an older, wiser friend and asked for his guidance. He said, "You're addicted to matches. It's exciting to be with these matches, but they go out and always need to be relit. You like that challenge. But what you need is a furnace, someone that doesn't always need to be relit."

I immediately saw the truth in his words. As long as I remained fascinated by matches, I would keep overlooking the furnaces. I needed to look inside and examine this pattern that kept me split between what I said I wanted on one hand and what I did on the other. A month, later I had my first date with a furnace, my future husband, Hugh.

I'll explain this further with an example of an overweight client who came to see me. She told me she had tried every diet and fast, but none of them worked for her. By shifting her focus away from her eating habits, we were able to move into her interior, where she finally faced the aspect of herself that was resistant and unwilling to become thin. Soon after these Releasing sessions, she was able to achieve the results her heart desired because it was now a unified self that was dieting and exercising.

Part Two, The Workbook, focuses on The Ten Hindrances to Your Heart's Desires, and is an invitation to expose that concealed part of yourself to the light of day. There is always a way out of the darkness, and the processes offered in the next section are meant to do just that. This excavating work will precipitate a vital change in your life. It will bring you into integrity and wholeness. We have discovered an important truth:

The degree to which people prevent fulfillment in their lives can be measured by the degree to which they conceal themselves.

Let's talk about the word "conceal." The dictionary meaning offers some clues as to how this type of hindrance operates:

> *conceal:* to keep from being seen, found, observed, or discovered; hide.
> Verb: 1. To prevent (something) from being known. Cover, hide, veil, mask, shroud, cloak, enshroud. 2. To put or keep out of sight. Hide, bury, ensconce, secrete, stash, cache.

After many years of facilitating all types of people through a variety of situations, we have seen one constant truth: A certain kind of willingness is required on the client's part, a courageous willingness to no longer conceal. As you prepare to launch into your own inner experience, it will be useful to look in on two scenarios that demonstrate how this can play out.

Scenario #1: As Hugh and I are facilitating a Releasing group, Mary describes an issue that is going on in her life. However, as she talks, we notice an uneasiness and restlessness in the room. It's apparent to me that an undeveloped, manipulative aspect of Mary is talking. It's an unconscious pattern she has, and it seems to be causing a chill in the room. When I tell Mary that I am aware she is speaking from a manip- ulative place, Mary responds, "I am? Really? I know that I've pushed people away, and if this has anything to do with that, I want to know." She then looks toward the group and asks them, "How do you see this in me?"

Having opened the door, Mary listens as people tell her their experi- ence of feeling manipulated by her. Mary begins to connect with a pain- ful memory of the time when she decided that the only way she felt she could be on top was to manipulate. The Releasing Process concludes with Mary feeling free of this life-long pattern that often kept her sepa- rate from others. Elapsed time: thirty-five minutes.

Scenario #2: Mary is told the same thing about her manipulative aspect and reacts by saying, "I feel judged. I don't think you really understand me or that you are hearing me correctly. Why can't you just accept me for the way I am?" The more that people in the group reach out to Mary, the more she pushes them away and acts defensive. She insists it's about her not being understood.

Many people like Mary settle for being understood rather than being seen. They spend most of their units of time and energy trying to be understood. This takes a huge toll on their ability to really go after and create what they say they want. When we continue to hide who we are from others—and from ourselves—we run, we defend, and armor our- selves, hoping that we never get found out.

Because the group loves Mary and sees how she has painted herself into a corner, we stick with it until she eventually sees that she is caught up in her fear, her strategies, and her no. She thanks the group and pro- ceeds through the Releasing part of the program. Elapsed time: two hours.

In one of our groups, a participant once said to me, "Boy, I can't hide anything from you, can I?" I responded, "Why would you want to?"

And here is another definition:

reveal: 1. to make known something concealed or secret. To bring to view, lay open, expose, unveil, unmask. 2. To make known by supernatural or divine means.

We now invite you, the reader, to enter into The Workbook, summoning your courageous willingness to reveal yourself as we approach The Ten Hindrances to Your Heart's Desires.

II

The Workbook

Hindrance: Anything that impedes or prevents entry or passage

If you advance confidently in the direction of your dreams, and endeavor to live the life you have imagined, you will meet with the success unexpected in common hours. You will pass an invisible boundary...if you have built castles in the air, your work need not be lost; that is where they should be. Now put the foundation under them.

—Henry David Thoreau

"So tell me again—why does it take so much time for me to create the reality I choose?"

"For a number of reasons. Because you do not believe you can have what you choose. Because you do not know what to choose. Because you keep trying to figure out what's best for you. Because you want guarantees ahead of time that all your choices will be good and because you keep changing your mind!"

—Neale Donald Walsch
Conversations with God

6

Creating the Blueprint for Your Heart's Desires

We all know that every successful endeavor begins with a plan. This is true even for matters of the heart. Such a notion makes some people uncomfortable; they believe we should simply accept what comes and not mess with fate. Their discomfort, however, may also be a fear of the emotions that they sense will be triggered by writing down, in no uncertain terms, what they, in their heart of hearts, have secretly longed for their whole lives.

Years before we met, Hugh and I had each done a similar exercise, creating a shopping list of qualities we were looking for in our divine mate. A couple years after we fell in love, we rediscovered these lists and found that we had described each other to a T!

EXERCISE
Creating Your New Blueprint

Take a moment to peruse the topics listed on the blueprint that follows. Then follow this process:

1. Close your eyes. Take a few deep breaths. Quiet your mind.

2. Center your awareness and simply ask yourself the question, "What would make my heart sing regarding _____ _____ (relationship, career, or any other topic that is important to you) at this time?"

3. Using the blueprint form, write down at least three things you want to create that would make your heart sing.

4. Repeat the first three steps for each topic.

5. When you have completed the process, sign and date the form.

This exercise is an opportunity for you to create the new blueprint for how you desire your life to unfold. Make sure that it corresponds to who you are *becoming*, because often what we ask for are hand-me-downs of who we once were.

Doubt, fears, and the ego's no may begin to surface as soon as you begin the exercise. Let them be there, but continue to fill out as much as you can under each topic.

MY NEW BLUEPRINT

LIFE PURPOSE
1.
2.
3.

CAREER
1.
2.
3.

RELATIONSHIPS (ALL TYPES)
1.
2.
3.

HEALTH
1.
2.
3.

PERSONAL GROWTH
1.
2.
3.

SPIRITUAL GROWTH
1.
2.
3.

OTHER
1.
2.
3

In order to create these outcomes in my life, I want to know specifically what hinders and obstructs my way.

_____ (Your Signature)

_____ (Date)

You now have in front of you your current wish list for virtually every aspect of your life. With this list in hand, begin reading through the Ten Hindrances to create the list of your heart's desires.

You are now ready to turn the page and face what hinders you.

7

Introduction to
The Ten Hindrances

While facilitating a workshop and uncovering the potential in the current life challenges facing a participant, we often arrive at a familiar place where the solution or epiphany hasn't yet landed in the heart of that person. It's an uncomfortable and frustrating situation. At this point, they will sometimes look to us for the answer. They want us to tell them *their* truth, which by definition we cannot do. We can only allude to the truth through stories and metaphors, but even then, it is not their personal experience of the truth of who they are at their core with all their unique beauty and potential.

What we can do, however, is come through the back door and tell them what *isn't* their truth. What becomes obvious through our interaction, are the ways they are not acting authentically, the fears and beliefs that are running their lives, and the denial of their purpose in being on this planet. Naturally, this can be very uncomfortable to hear, so we try to proceed with as much compassion and humor as we can. But as we explained earlier, in order to be our best, we must first be willing to face our worst.

The Ten Hindrances to Your Heart's Desires, which you are about to consider, come directly from these group situations with our clients. There is a universality to the anecdotes and stories shared here, and they are valuable learning tools. By bringing a quality of honest self-inquiry to the processes offered here, you can leave behind old habits and behaviors that have stood in the way of you living your truth. You can be freed to pursue the path in life that makes your heart sing!

The Ten Hindrances are:

1. Lack of clarity

2. Complaints, excuses, stories, and dramas about how it doesn't work for you because you're special

3. Unwillingness to take responsibility

4. Fear of owning your own power

5. Lack of impeccability

6. Unwillingness to forgive

7. Fear of the Light

8. Hating the physical

9. Inability to trust existence

10. Unwillingness to serve

Many of the case studies are composites of our clients, whose names have been changed. We offer their stories not to expose or embarrass them in any way, but to give you an opportunity to see yourself in their stories.

8

Hindrance #1:
Lack of Clarity

You can't get what you want 'til you know what you want.

—from the song *You Can't Get What You Want* by Joe Jackson

Only a conscious intention can plant and nurture the seeds for our dreams and visions to blossom in the physical realm—and clarity is what fuels that intention. However, since we're not conscious of everything that motivates us, what often prevents clarity from fueling our vision are all of our unconscious fears and programs subverting that vision behind the scenes.

For instance, have you ever tried to bring a great idea or plan to fruition only to feel frustration and disappointment at the results? Somehow, something gets lost in the execution, or you feel like you're being sabotaged. It slowly dawns on you that you may also have unconscious intentions at work. It's as if two minds are operating without consulting one another. On one hand, you have clarity about what you want, but when you set it all in motion, another voice or influence with a negative tone throws in the proverbial monkey wrench.

Ernie Els is a world-class golfer who has won two U.S. Open titles. Undoubtedly, he is a man with great confidence in his ability to perform under pressure, but he said that when Tiger Woods rose to prominence, he began to doubt himself. He said, "I had a little man on my shoulder that told me I couldn't pull off a certain golf shot, and sure enough, I'd mess it up." He went from being number one in the world to losing to Tiger, time and time again. His desire to win was never in question, but he was still undermining himself with his unconscious intentions, symbolized by the little man and his feeling intimidated by Tiger.

There is no better catalyst for bringing our unconscious intentions to the surface than a passionate desire to have a dream come true. That passion evokes a tenuous meeting between the conscious and unconscious, where the world that exists behind our eyes collides with the world in front of our eyes.

When we have a heart's desire to create success in the outer world, we are in effect putting out an invitation for Existence to bring to the surface all obstacles and barriers that stand in the way of our success. But this is not a bad thing. We are asking Existence to bring these hindrances to the surface so they can be transformed, so they no longer have the power to cripple us as they have in the past. When we counsel couples, we see a similar dynamic in the early stages of love. As the pink glow of infatuation fades, irritating habits and petty squabbles make them wonder if it's the beginning of the end of their relationship. We explain to the exasperated couple a metaphysical truth that is simply a part of this getting-to-know-you phase:

Love brings up everything unlike itself to be cleansed.

When Hugh and I were falling in love, there were times when I felt like I had never been loved so much. I would feel anxious and perhaps even pick a fight just to get away from the intensity of the love. He also needed to retreat into his cave at times. We soon realized that there was nothing wrong with us—all this love was just unfamiliar. During these moments, I discovered that it was helpful for me to say to him, "Honey, stop loving me right now because I can't take it anymore." For the first few months of our relationship, this little sentence was of great value. When it would become too intense, instead of needing to look for a problem I could just say, "Honey, stop loving me right now because I can't take it anymore." It was like the out breath of our love, and in the next breath, I could take in a little more love. Sometimes just by saying it, and acknowledging the truth of the situation, something would free up inside me, and I could relax then and there. When you start to identify your style of responding or your particular limits, you can acknowledge them, love yourself, and begin to look for ways you can stretch a little bit more the next time.

Hugh had not been in a committed relationship for almost ten years when we first got together. He had become so used to sleeping alone that it was hard for him to sleep in physical contact with me. His heart would beat faster, and he'd feel anxious and restless. He acknowledged that the combination of physical and emotional intimacy that we were exploring felt scary and a little threatening. But he took it as a challenge rather than a reason to quit, and over the weeks and months, we experimented with more and more contact until finally he could relax and enjoy "spooning" for the entire night. I might add that in a situation like this a woman can find it difficult to not take it personally.

Richard

Richard came for a session a year ago and was excited about a men's support group he wanted to start. I was concerned that he was proceeding too quickly, but he insisted that he was ready. The first meeting with the men blew up in his face. He had read everyone in the group his agenda and wanted to proceed, but several men took issue with his style and demeanor. Richard became defensive and tried to dismiss what they were saying. It all went downhill from there, disintegrating into arguments and ill will. Of course, this was very discouraging for Richard, and he needed a couple of sessions with me just to decompress from the trauma of it all! When he looked more deeply into it, he realized that smoldering, unresolved issues from his childhood had been ignited by his attempt to become a group facilitator. He continued to unravel his old issues and began to understand where he'd gone wrong in the workshop. He phoned me a few months later, delighted to share his success with the group and how he'd become neutral and empowered around those issues that had previously stopped him.

When we notice that trying to create something in our life starts a process that invites everything to the surface that impedes our progress, we open a door for true miracles to occur. There's a natural tendency to fight those negative thoughts and programs in an attempt to overpower or eliminate them. Ironically, that kind of attention feeds the negativity and actually makes it stronger. By not fighting or denying it, but simply by acknowledging and observing it, we make it possible for that negative energy to be transformed into a positive outcome. With The Releasing Process, we allow ourselves to feel those repressed emotions. The energy lightens and changes within us. The fear, resignation, and confusion are transformed into the positive energy of trust, confidence, and clarity.

Even in the world of professional sports, we can see examples of this dynamic at work. In a recent interview, Ernie Els said he tried to improve his game by hitting golf balls for six hours a day, "...but that didn't help. I then began to think about my attitude, which wasn't good, and I went to a sports psychologist. Instead of fighting my fear, he had me observe it. He had me take my attention off of Tiger and focus on my own game. Now I kind of feel like I'm really back. I want to dream big again." A month later, Ernie defeated Tiger Woods and the rest of the field to win his third major tournament, the 2002 British Open.

Lack of Clarity is the number one hindrance on our list because so few people understand how pivotal it is in thwarting our creative output and success in the world. So often, I've seen the sad resignation in the eyes of a client—not to mention the layers of resignation I see clairvoyantly in their energy bodies.

They may also carry the pain of broken promises made by well-intentioned teachers, who insist that if we simply harness our will power, we can do anything we want with our life. Infomercials on TV seduce us with get-rich-quick techniques and schemes. The fact is, very few of us can "personal power" our way to success like a Tony Robbins.

Although muscling your way through all obstacles with mindforce seems like an obvious way to achieve one's goals ("achieve" being the operative word here), that approach does not require you to go into the nooks and crannies of the unconscious, and therefore any positive results simply feed the ego rather then nourish the soul.

I know how scary it can be to invite God-knows-what up to the surface to be confronted and then healed. But summoning the courage to go through this process brings a new-found freedom that allows the soul to soar to new heights. Remember, we do not bring up painful or difficult feelings in order to dwell on the past or blame our parents. We do it so that the negative energy of past traumas and disappointments can be transmuted into the fuel and creative energy of your present dreams and heart's desires.

There is a specific type of clarity that I wish to discuss; it is the clarity of understanding what stops us from having our heart's desires. This can feel daunting at first, but we found a key phrase that would always bring us back to clarity:

When you go to your purpose, your confusion dissolves.

If we are unsure or lack clarity about what we want, then whatever we create in our life remains vague. The old beliefs and patterns must be neutralized so they no longer act as a hindrance. Whether it's clarity on our mission in this life, whom we are to serve, our relationship to another person, or how to proceed with a venture, the process of achieving clarity requires us to become conscious of what hinders us.

Otherwise, we may become frustrated and bored, resigned to a life of unfulfilled dreams and aborted plans. Without making definite conscious choices, we are submitting to the results of our unconscious choices or other peoples' choices. To succeed at what we want in life, we must become utterly clear on what our heart desires. In reaching this state of clarity, we must ask ourselves a crucial question:

"What is my purpose?"

We can start with something as basic as our relationships. Reflect for a moment and ask yourself, "What is my purpose in being friends with so-and-so?" Is this a friendship that supports, inspires, brings joy, and nourishes you, or are the two of you merely killing time and adding new meaning to the expression "Misery loves company"? Or even worse, have you chosen to surround yourself with acquaintances who mirror your cynicism and defeatism? Carolyn Myss coined a phrase for two people who have this type of dysfunctional arrangement. She calls them "wound-mates." A fiercely honest inventory of our friendships can make us aware that if our lives are to change and evolve for the better, we need to bid farewell to friendships that no longer support who we are becoming.

All of our classes begin with a statement of the group's purpose. It is important that we do this because Releasing work invites up all the unconscious garbage that is in the way of the participants' inner healing and outer success. Consequently, it often feels quite intense and disturbing in the room. One day, during one of our six-month groups, almost every participant entered the room saying, "I don't want to be here today." The stubbornness and resistance in the room was palpable. Closing our eyes for a moment and tuning in to Spirit, I received a gentle reminder to share with the group: "The more one chooses to go toward their truth and the Light, the more their ego will clamor." Having the participants reread the group purpose eventually quieted the childish and fearful no that had been pervading the room.

This is why it is so important to have your purpose anchored firmly in your heart. The heart is an ally of our Being, and it is capable of offsetting the noise of the ego/mind, whose main functions are to resist change, avoid risks, and enforce the status quo. We have witnessed egos create flat tires, babysitters canceling, and mysterious sudden sickness, all because the ego is afraid of what it might hear in class. One man suddenly found himself with an annoying earache just before a workshop. To his credit, he endured it, and came anyway. The moment he heard the truth about his situation and then released what was needed, his earache disappeared! So we repeat:

When you go to your purpose, your confusion dissolves.

To further illustrate how this principle operates in people's lives, I'll explain how we apply it in couple counseling. When working with couples, we find they often get stuck in the muck of blame, guilt, and anger. Preoccupied with the details of their problems, they've lost touch with their original purpose in coming together. Having them dig out and reread their marriage vows helps them to rise above their bickering and view their marriage from the higher, more spiritual perspective that they felt in their hearts on their wedding day. This, in turn, opens up a space in which they can hear each other with patience and a renewed commitment. Of course it sometimes makes them realize they no longer share the same vision. They may then decide to end their relationship—but then that happens from a place of mutual respect and understanding, instead of a position of recrimination and hatred.

When Hugh and I married, we knew we wanted to work together, serving humanity to the best of our ability. We sat down and created a contract with Spirit, elaborating from our hearts what our purpose was in doing this work. When we didn't have immediate success in the outer world, doubts and fears would arise, but staying focused on our purpose bolstered and inspired us time after time. Writing that original contract was a real stretch for us, but discovering it in our files years later, we were amazed that we had accomplished virtually everything in it.

When planning workshops, we always consult Spirit to see if proceeding is in the highest good of ourselves and all concerned. Our first weekend residential was planned for a beautiful coastal location in California called Sea Ranch, and we felt aligned with Spirit. But when I talked to a dear friend about participating, she said, "I would love to come, but a friend is getting married that weekend. Can you change it to the weekend before the wedding?" My mind began to scheme, thinking, "Well she's *got* to be there, so I'll switch the dates." I then remembered my purpose is to be surrendered to Spirit and receive guidance there, not from people with a scheduling conflict. When I spoke with her again, I told her the date would remain the same. If she could make it, fine—otherwise, perhaps the next time. After some reflection, she chose to attend our workshop, realizing that it was in *her* highest good, whereas the wedding had merely been an obligation to an old friend with whom she no longer truly felt connected.

Even if you are very certain about your purpose, it is possible to be thrown off balance by well-intended advice or so-called conventional wisdom. In the early days when work was slow, our own self-doubts caused us confusion. So we'd try to figure out, "What does the public want; what do they need?" None of that truly matters, however, if you believe in yourself and your inner gifts. By continually tuning in to your innermost truth, vision, and purpose, you are tuning into universal truths to which everyone can relate. The more you remain aligned with your purpose, the more Existence aligns with you. The following passage illustrates this beautifully:

> Until one is committed,
> There is hesitancy, the chance to draw back,
> always ineffectiveness.
>
> Concerning acts of initiative (and creation)
> There is one elementary truth
> the ignorance of which kills countless ideas
> and splendid plans:
>
> That the moment one definitely commits oneself
> then Providence moves too.
>
> All sorts of things occur to help one
> That would never otherwise have occurred.
>
> A whole stream of events issues from the decision,
> Raising in one's favor all manner
> of unforeseen incidents and meetings

and material assistance
Which no person could have dreamt
would come their way.

Whatever you can do, or dream you can, begin it.
Boldness has genius, power and magic in it.

Begin it now.

—Goethe

Another way we are deterred from our purpose is by listening to an aspect of ourselves we call the spiritual rationalizer. Most people embody this characteristic in varying degrees, ranging from vague superstitions to highly sophisticated belief systems. For example, a client of ours was attempting to sell her business for several months, with no success. Her spiritual explanation was, "I guess this is a sign that the universe doesn't want me to sell it." However, when we dug a little deeper with her, we found there were ways she was holding on to the business, of which she was unaware. We had her release it, and sure enough, two weeks later, the business was sold. We have had many "spiritual" clients who try to convince themselves they no longer have any earthly desires and simply want to "surrender" to Existence. More often than not, what they are calling surrender is actually a form of resignation, and a turning away from life and the gifts they have to offer. The spiritual component of hindrances to our heart's desires is explored further in upcoming chapters.

What is your soul's purpose? Many of us have inflated ideas concerning our mission here on Earth, while others feel their lives are inconsequential. Some people think it's their job to save the whales, when actually they're in need of saving themselves.

Regina

A woman came to me recently because she was experiencing very real survival fears. She was in a panic. When I began to facilitate her, what came to the surface to be released was very revealing. We uncovered lifetime after lifetime in which Regina had become homeless and destitute. She feared that her soul's purpose was to learn some spiritual lesson that could only be accomplished by being homeless. She had a very sophisticated spiritual rationalizer in her mind, convincing her that being homeless would be the high road for her to take. During the session, she relived past lives when she'd been mistreated by the wealthy, resulting in her current judgments of the rich and her romanticized notions of being more spiritual and closer to God than they were. (One clue that the spiritual rationalizer is at work is that there is an "us versus them" component to the scenario.) It was a watershed session for her, and her irrational fears of ending up homeless were resolved. Regina soon found a comfortable place to live, and is now working in a satisfying job, no longer waiting for the other shoe to drop.

Adopting a social cause and calling it our purpose is like mixing oil and water. A cause usually carries with it a political agenda with stated or implied enemies. We are encouraged to take an adversarial stance toward the so-called enemies of our cause and divorce ourselves from our heart. Remembering that our purpose must be anchored in our heart, we realize we are literally at cross-purposes.

Few people manage to successfully balance a social cause with their purpose. The challenge is to not throw the opponents of our cause out of our heart. A cause is best pursued with a calm, workmanlike quality. A Zen teacher would encourage the protester to conduct his protest as if he were simply "chopping wood and carrying water from the well."

Your purpose is very different from your goals. Goals are determined by the mind and fueled by willpower. They can be useful, but are comparatively superficial. Purpose originates in a deeper, more heart-centered source of our Being. When you act from your purpose, you have a clarity and direction that allows you to rise above the old cynicism, self-doubt, and confusion. Goals may also be imposed by a family or culture.

Imagine that your heart's desire and soul purpose in this lifetime is to be a jazz singer, but you've been raised in a family of lawyers and find yourself enrolled in law school. You would have to cut yourself off from your heart in order to make it through each semester, living a very conflicted life.

Are you doing the work that you came to this planet to accomplish? It is no accident that you are on this planet here and now. You have a mission, a gift to share, a purpose in being here.

Even if you are now working at a job only for the paycheck, it's important to begin the inner process of identifying your purpose, so you can eventually make the transition into doing your true work. It is possible to find a new depth of meaning or higher lesson in that routine job—perhaps in the quality you bring to your contact with clients or fellow employees. And watch for clues that indicate the direction you need to take to bring you more in touch with living your purpose.

In the movie *Jerry Maguire,* the main character becomes disillusioned with the callous and ruthless nature of his profession. An inner voice calls out to him about a new way to do his work. He is so inspired, he stays up all night writing his mission statement. The rest of the movie unfolds his struggle with inner and outer demons that test his commitment to remaining true to his purpose. This film is a visually rich example of how periods of confusion are an inevitable part of the process. The conclusion of the movie reinforces the fact that "When you go to your purpose, your confusion dissolves."

EXERCISE
Discovering Your Purpose

Knowing what you want is the first step in drawing your purpose toward you.

We will now take you through a process to assist you in becoming clear on your purpose. The exercise is designed to put you in touch with the world that exists "behind your eyes." Read the instructions and then decide on the best way for you to engage in the process.

1. Close your eyes, take a few slow, deep breaths, and focus your awareness in your heart. Inside your heart a seed was planted a long time ago. This seed represents the essence of your purpose. You may already be familiar with the seed or you may be noticing it for the first time. Can you see what is it? Look and see what stage of development this seedling is in. Has it sprouted? Has it been watered recently or is it in need of nourishment?

2. Now ask Spirit Most High to take you back in time to when your seed was planted. Ask Spirit to now show you the nature of that seed, taking you into the very core of it that holds your soul purpose in this lifetime. Look at it from as many angles as possible. When you're finished, open your eyes.

3. You are now ready to write out your personal mission statement, your purpose. For now, keep it simple and to the point.

EXERCISE
Creating Your Personal Mission Statement

To give you an idea, here is ours: Our purpose at Toward Wholeness is service. We assist others to release the density that binds them so they can move toward wholeness in mind, body, and Spirit and experience their own divinity, so that they may live the life that makes their heart sing!

Now write out yours.

My Personal Mission Statement

Signature_____

Date_____

RELEASING PROCESS

Larry was a young real estate agent who moonlighted as a piano player in a bar. He shared with us that this was a guilty pleasure that his family didn't know about. Delving a little deeper, it seems that Larry had been discouraged by his parents to pursue a musical career. Close to tears, he finally allowed that music had always been his first love and he dreamed of succeeding as a jazz pianist.

Below are the key elements we had him release. Repeat them for yourself or write them out. Adapt those statements that may not feel specific to you, so they reflect your situation.

- I release all pacts and agreements I made with my mother (and/or) father to ignore my purpose and follow what they think is my purpose.

- I release thinking and believing that if I follow their plan, I may win their love and approval.

- I release the sadness in my heart for not being true to my purpose.

- I ask the God within me to clear all obstacles and barriers in the way of seeing clearly what my mission is here on Earth.

- I release any fear of seeing what my mission is here on Earth.

- I release running from Spirit on the astral* every time I am shown what my mission is here on Earth.

- I release my fear of taking on my mission because I think and believe that I'm not worthy of it.

- I release all unforgiveness toward myself for not being further along in accomplishing my mission

- I release my habit of running from myself on the astral.

- I now turn around and face the part of me I've been running from.

- I release the effects of the exhaustion from the years of running from myself, when I was unwilling to face that part of me I hold to be unlovable, unworthy, undeserving, damaged.

- I release the decision I made that I could never have what I've always wanted.

- I ask the God within to put me in touch with my purpose, more and more each day.

*It is important to understand that we are all multidimensional beings. For example, we dwell simultaneously on the spiritual, emotional, and physical planes. We are continually influenced by these other dimensions. Another plane where we exist is the astral. The astral plane bridges the physical and the spiritual dimensions and is a realm in which we are acting out unfulfilled fears and fantasies. For an entertaining explanation of the astral, see the movie *Flatliners*, in which the netherworld before death is a fairly accurate representation of the astral plane. The Releasing Process addresses these other planes and dimensions where we also exist.

9

Hindrance #2:
Complaints, Excuses, Stories, and Dramas about
How It Doesn't Work for You
Because You're Special

Past the wounds of childhood, past the fallen dreams and the broken families, through the hurt and the loss and the agony only the night ever hears, is a waiting soul. Patient, permanent, abundant; it opens its infinite heart and asks only one thing of you. Remember who it is you really are.

—Karen Alexander and Rick Boyes, *Losing Your Mind*

We enjoy sharing the stories of how people's lives have been transformed through The Releasing Process. However, not everyone has the same results. Several clients have been so invested in their stories, and all the perks and attention they received, that they couldn't let them go.

Janice
Janice came to me complaining that she had been unable to sell her house for more than a year. This was in Marin County, a very hot real

estate market. As she recited to me, giving me all these great reasons why it wasn't working for her, I could see a deep-seated belief inside her that success will always elude her. When I explained that I was seeing this in her energy field, she retorted sarcastically, "Well that's an interesting theory!"

I saw that her mind was too much in control to accept what I was saying, so I had to try a different and more experiential approach. I had her stand across the room from me. I said to her, "Imagine that I am Existence. I want to meet you and give you whatever you want. I just need for you to meet me." Stepping closer to her, again I said, "Meet me. You just have to meet me halfway." I stepped closer, whispering, "Meet me." I was now almost touching her body, and she hadn't moved. I then said very gently, "Meet me." She began to tremble, started sobbing, and finally said, "I can't! I don't know how." I then did some releasing with Janice, which is included at the end of this chapter.

Many years ago, even I had a great story about how family dealings with my money had left me broke. I could have received much sympathy and agreement about my financial woes, but I knew that I had to give up my story in order to expand my own financial horizons.

You can either have your story or you can have transformation, but you can't have both.

The downside of many New Age and spiritual teachings is that they can be breeding grounds for people to develop offbeat stories and excuses about how it doesn't work for them because they're special. For example, valuable lessons can be learned through astrology and other metaphysical systems, but this knowledge can also be used to reinforce self-limiting beliefs and ideas about one's life.

Suzanne and Joe

My favorite example of this was a couple who attended our relationship workshop, *Two Wings To God*. There was much love between Suzanne and Joe, but also glaring differences in how each approached life. In a private session during the weekend, they explained to me what they believed was the real reason why Joe couldn't fully commit to their relationship. It seems that a few years before, a psychic had told him that Joe had a hard time making up his mind about being born, but also felt an urgency from his angels that he must incarnate at that time because his service was needed. However, his hasty birth caused him to skip some important lessons, making him unable to be fully present and take on commitments, such as relationships.

As Joe explained his dilemma to me, Suzanne sat with big, compassionate eyes, perhaps thinking that since I was so intuitive, I would be enrolled in this story, as she had been, and I would understand! This type of "understanding" in a relationship is the consolation prize. When Joe finished his story, I looked at Suzanne and asked, "And you buy this—that the reason he can't marry you is because he missed some classes before he was born?"

At first, she was shocked that I wasn't sympathetic to Joe's plight, but after some discussion, she realized she'd been under the spell of a New Age fairy tale. Joe had convinced himself and her of how spiritual he was. The whole scenario had merely reinforced Suzanne's pattern of not standing up for what she wanted.

It is sad to see someone so wounded or overlooked early in life that he or she was never allowed to feel special, unique, or gifted. In adulthood, such a person tries to feel special through their pain and drama. But a story is only useful when others can be enrolled in it, giving the person some attention or energy. This pattern keeps them marinating in the juices of their drama, spinning an endless tape loop that keeps them stuck in their egocentric world. If they could only see how much it's costing them emotionally, spiritually, and physically, they'd be inclined to drop their story. Zen teacher Suzuki Roshi saw this tendency in some of his students and called them dharma-ridden, meaning that these meditators had spiritual pride standing in the way of true spiritual advancement.

I remember as a child often being annoyed with my mother. After my car accident, no matter where she went or whom she met, in less than five minutes she would work into the conversation that she had a daughter with one leg. I was too young to understand that my mother had never felt special and now she had her chance. I just knew I felt queasy seeing her get attention from people in this way. I also saw that the price of this attention was that it caused her to relive the accident over and over again, which had a debilitating effect on her. As with others who get caught up in this hindrance, my mother would invariably create even more dramas in her life, because she learned that this was how to get attention, sympathy, and a feeling of importance. Seeing my mother act this way sent me to the other extreme. I would never mention my leg or allow it to interfere with my life—to a fault. However, through the Releasing work, I have found balance in this aspect of my life.

EXERCISE
Eliminating Excuses, Stories, and Dramas

1. For one week, use the chart below to keep a diary of excuses and rationalizations you've told yourself or others about why you couldn't rise to the occasion or keep a commitment.

2. On a scale of 1 to 10, how often are you enrolling people in your story?

3. On a scale of 1 to 10, how successful are you in enrolling them in your story?

Day #	Excuses You Have Told Yourself and Others	Are You Enrolling Others?	How Successful Are You?

RELEASING PROCESS

• I release my disappointment about the times I didn't succeed at something that I hoped would make me feel special.

• I release the layers upon layers of resignation from thinking and believing I would never succeed.

• I release my fear that I would never feel special.

• I release the effects of the sympathy and attention I got when I didn't succeed.

• I release the decision I made to cling to the story of how I don't succeed.

• I release my belief that my story makes me special.

• I release my attachment to my stories.

• I release my conviction that what happened to me in the past still prevents me from pursuing my heart's desires.

• I release all the limitations I've imposed on myself with the stories and excuses in my life.

• I release the shock and sadness I feel when I acknowledge the ways I've remained in my comfort zone.

• I release all unforgiveness toward myself for preferring my story to pursuing my dreams.

• I ask the God within to give me the courage to break free of this pattern and go for my highest good.

10

Hindrance #3: Unwillingness to Take Responsibility

There are no accidents. Everything that happens is part of the infinite divine plan unfolding. Your freedom lies in your ability to accept and to respond to the situation as it is.

—Sabina Pettitt, *Energy Medicine*

We had an acquaintance named James, and whenever something happened in his circle of friends that seemed to be a bad thing, his first thought was always, 'I wonder why they created that in their life'. On the surface, it seems like a reasonable response for someone on a spiritual path, but it also feels very unloving. In fact, it was more like an accusation based on a notion of what a truth seeker should be asking themselves. The irony is that whenever life threw James a curve, he'd avoid acknowledging it was his creation and instead he'd meet the situation with a sense of shame. In other words, he was proud of his "good" creations, while his "bad" creations made him feel shame.

Shame and pride are by-products of our ego's insistence on certain results. As we evolve in consciousness, we become less caught up by these polarities and open up to a higher learning about our creations.

How do you respond when Existence throws you a curve? Do you feel ashamed when something "bad" happens to you? Does it make you feel guilty? Do you feel victimized by "bad" things happening in your life or are you able to enjoy the freedom that comes from being able to respond to the situation as it is?

The question, "Why did they create that?" is not necessarily the wrong question; it depends on where the question originates. Is the question coming from the Higher or the lower Self? Only when it is asked from the Higher Self will there be a response that can lead to clarity and peace of mind. When you accept that you've chosen life experiences in order to learn, you will be truly free.

I haven't always known this for myself, but I seem to have recognized it on a cellular level when I lost my leg in the car accident. I even remember as a little girl, years before the accident, getting up in the middle of the night and practicing standing on one leg, in case I ever lost my leg. My gradual acceptance of what happened to me made all the difference in the world in my recovery. And I was empowered from the experience rather then victimized. As I said, I haven't always embraced my accountability, so whenever I've forgotten that I'm a willing participant and have resisted, my responses led to pain, whether it was physical, emotional, or psychic.

Another way we avoid responsibility is by hanging on to an emotional charge regarding somebody or something. At times, we may become incredibly irritated and even hateful toward someone. Feeling something strongly and freely expressing it can be very healthy—for example, when you've been cut off in traffic and you vent your frustration with a juicy swear word.

The trick, of course, is in letting it go and moving on, not allowing the emotion to take us over and become road rage. The problem is that at that point, the lower self is running the show, and it's hard to believe that there could be a lesson for us in a situation when all we see is red. Thus begins a very challenging tightrope act. If we remain in our anger, we miss the lesson and are left only with the curse of our anger churning our insides. However, if we cut off our emotions and convince ourselves we "understand" the other driver, telling ourselves that he was probably beaten as a child, we swing to the other extreme. We need to allow our emotions to be present and uncensored, but bring just enough awareness to say to ourselves, "I really hate what's happening right now, but I'm going to somehow find a way to be open to whatever lesson is here for me."

This slows down the sequence of events and opens up the possibility for our Higher Self to see the entire drama, with all the players, and ask, "What can I learn from this?" In contrast, it is our lower self and its judging mind that causes us the most pain.

This is well illustrated in a story from the days of Lao Tzu in China taken from the *Osho Transformation Tarot*:

> *An old man living in a village was very poor and his only true asset was a beautiful white horse. One day the horse was gone. The villagers gathered and said, "You foolish old man! You could have sold that horse for a fortune and now you have nothing. What a misfortune!" The old man said, "Don't go so far as to say that. Simply say that the horse is not in the stable. This is the fact; everything else is a judgment. Whether it is a misfortune or a blessing I don't know, who knows what will follow?"*
>
> *People laughed at the old man, but fifteen days later the horse returned, and not only that, he brought a dozen wild horses with him. Again the villagers gathered and said, "Old man you were right, this was not a misfortune, it has indeed proven to be a blessing." The man said, "Just say that the horse is back. Who knows if it is a blessing?" This time the people could not say much, but inside they knew he was wrong. Twelve beautiful horses had come.*
>
> *The old man's son began training the horses but fell and broke both his legs. Again the villagers came and claimed it was a misfortune: "Your son was your only support in your old age. Now you are poorer than ever." And the old man replied, "Nobody knows this. Life comes in fragments and more is never given to you."*
>
> *After a few weeks the country went to war and all the town's young men were forcibly taken by the military. They knew that most of their sons would never return so they went to the old man and said, "You are so lucky that your son's legs were broken and he wasn't sent to war."*

Of course, we know the old man's response.

Until we release our belief that everything in our life is either good or bad, a success or a failure, we miss out on so many of the wonderful and mysterious lessons that life brings our way. Another way of saying this is that when life doesn't match our hopes or expectations, we feel shamed and beaten down by the challenges and we recoil from and resist their lessons.

A friend of ours was recently injured in a serious car accident. His car was struck head-on by a careless teenage driver who was speeding on the wrong side of the road. Our friend Ian was understandably upset and angry at this young man for completely altering his life physically, financially, and emotionally. Ian put himself through all of the usual mental torment: "Why me?"…"If I'd only been a few minutes late"…"I'm going to sue this kid and his whole family!"

But for years, Ian had been a spiritual seeker who was not content with superficial explanations or knee-jerk responses. After he simmered down and took a couple weeks of reflection, another question finally occurred to him: "Have I contributed to this incident in any way?"

He acknowledged to himself that he'd been pushing very hard to get as much accomplished at work as he could so that he'd have more free time; but no matter how hard he pushed, he never seemed to get ahead time-wise. He also saw how proud he'd become at managing and controlling the many facets of his life. However, he'd been neglecting a deeper commitment to bring Spirit and his Higher Self into more of a managerial position in his life.

So Ian began to get the bigger picture around his accident, seeing how perhaps it was the universe's way of saying, "You deserve a break today." He saw how his forced convalescence was actually a gift of time—time to rest, reflect, and reprioritize his life. He was also thankful that a much more traumatic event was not required to get his attention.

When you reflect on your life, are you aware of incidents, patterns, habits for which you are unwilling to take responsibility? Do you tend to see your life as a collection of random incidents? Do you have a tendency to look outside of yourself for the cause?

The word "responsibility" often carries with it the notion of blame or burden so many people tend to avoid responsibility at all costs. They may take an aggressive, adversarial approach to life, needing to blame others for the circumstances of their life. A variation on this theme is the victim approach, where a person feels constantly set upon and blames everything from their upbringing to evil spirits for their problems. This is one of the reasons our society has become so litigious.

A life dedicated to the avoidance of responsibility is a major hindrance in creating a life of fulfillment be it career, relationship, or creativity.

Granted, the average person is fairly willing to take responsibility in everyday situations. For example, he'll willingly share the expense when a new fence is required between him and his neighbor. The irresponsible neighbor, on the other hand, will try to avoid the expense, claiming that the old fence is fine or will say, "Pay for it yourself if you think we need a new fence!"

What we are referring to in this chapter is a higher form of responsibility that requires us to be utterly honest with ourselves. When we embrace the possibility that we are responsible for everything in our life, right down to the choice of our family when we incarnated, it opens up a rich vista of connections and lessons. When we perceive our life from the perspective of our Higher Self, we see that virtually everything that transpires in our life has a connection or significance and that nothing is random or accidental. The rational mind is too pedestrian to appreciate this. It usually rebels at the very notion because what we're referring to is simply beyond its limited grasp.

No one can simultaneously take responsibility for their life and blame someone else.

What is required is a leap of trust. When we begin to trust that we really are always in the right place at the right time, our experiences finally make sense. After a seemingly accidental occurrence, it sometimes takes years to see the symmetry of certain events. But in retrospect, we can discern why it was all truly meant to be.

The ultimate lesson in responsibility for me came twenty years ago from my teacher, friend, and cousin, Waduda. During a workshop with her, I was blaming my mother for something she'd done to me. While ranting about the latest injustice I felt she had dealt me, and how I wanted to retaliate, Waduda looked me straight in the eyes and said, "You know, Voge, it is the responsibility of the more conscious person to resolve a situation."

It was as if a bolt of lightning went right through me! It took me at least five years to process that one sentence. Like so many, I wanted the perks of the spiritual journey without any of the responsibility. So, during those five years I went through periods of rebelling and hating this new "job." Sometimes I would even yell, "Why am I always the more conscious person in the situation?" I would go from feigning unconsciousness to posturing consciousness. Looking back, I can see that I was quite hilarious. Finally, I found some balance. In the heat of the moment, I may not always be as conscious as I'd like to be, but my *intention* is always to come from the heart and act responsibly to resolve the situation in an impeccable way.

A few years ago, Hugh was elected president of our homeowners association. Much ill will had been created in the community by the previous board members, and meetings were always tense and fraught with petty bickering that sometimes escalated into lawsuits. When Hugh began conducting the meetings, he would listen patiently and respectfully to each resident, regardless of how hostile or upset they were. He was then able to defuse the tension by including everyone in the room in a sincere discussion of how to proceed.

Hugh goes into every one of these meetings with the intention of resolving the issues from the most conscious space possible, from the space in which we are all one. As he likes to say, "After all, we are all bozos on this bus!" Since he has been in office, there has been quite a turnaround. Not only is everyone enjoying a friendlier, more relaxed atmosphere, but many residents who had stopped coming to those tense meetings are returning for the first time in years. Their re-involvement is creating a sense of community that many say they have longed for and now feel they are receiving. Everyone feels empowered now at the meetings. The "us versus them" tension is gone.

Taking responsibility in this way is the step one needs to take to own one's power, as you will learn in the next chapter.

EXERCISE
Uncovering the Cause

- Give yourself twenty minutes to complete this exercise.

- Close your eyes, center in your heart, and ask your Higher Self to be here with you now.

- Bring to mind an event in your life that has challenged you recently—one where you felt at the effect, perhaps even victimized.

- Ask yourself, "What are the negative thoughts and feelings I have that are causing this condition?"

- What are your "payoffs" for having this condition?

- What are your fears about giving up this condition?

- Now see yourself walking up a mountain with your Higher Self. As you climb, ask your Higher Self to show you the negative feeling and thought that are *most* responsible for creating this event in your life.

- When you get to the top, look down at the event from this higher perspective and ask to be shown the lesson you can learn through this experience.

- Say out loud: "I now choose to learn from this event."

- Be open to see what is being shown to you.

- When you come out of meditation, thank your Higher Self and the event for teaching you this lesson and affirm to yourself, "I got the lesson!"

- Repeat this exercise regarding any experiences from the past that are incomplete for you. Remember to affirm: "I got the lesson."

RELEASING PROCESS

- I release my insistence that I am a victim of circumstances.

- I release any residual blame I hold toward my parents, teachers, and bosses.

- I release any anger or blame toward God for relegating me to this planet and this life.

- I release my pattern of looking for the easy way out.

- I release my tendency to look for sympathy for how hard I've got it.

- I release listening to my lower self to justify feeling like a victim.

- I acknowledge that I have chosen this incarnation—every little bit of it.

- I release all unforgiveness toward others from my holding them accountable for what is actually my responsibility.

- I release all unforgiveness toward myself for ignoring my Higher Self and the lessons my Higher Self has been trying to give me.

11

Hindrance #4:
Fear of Owning Your Own Power

Authentic power comes from aligning personality with soul.

—Gary Zukav, *The Seat of the Soul*

This is the chapter in which so many of the other Hindrances combine into a united whole. When you are in your power, you have the *clarity* needed to stay on purpose, undeterred by outer circumstances. You are not run by the *stories, excuses, and dramas* of your past. You are able to *take responsibility* for all your creations without blame, judgments, or the need to self-punish. You act *impeccably*, truly walking your talk. *Forgiveness* occurs spontaneously because there is no longer a need to hang on to a grievance. You are a *force of Light* to be reckoned with—grounded in your *physicality, trusting* that all is in Divine Order, free of the ego's insistence that it needs to be his/her way. When you are in your power, your *service* has a greater capacity and is informed by your compassion.

When the war in Iraq broke out in 2003, author/psychiatrist Clarissa Pinkola Estes sent out a very powerful e-mail. She was reminding us all to stay in our power in these challenging times:

Do not lose heart. We were made for these times. For years we have been learning, been in training for a dark time such as this, since the day we assented to come to Earth...Didn't you say you pledged to listen to a Voice greater...?

As for me, little did I know that Waduda's suggestion about taking responsibility, referred to in the previous chapter, would put me on the path to owning my power more consciously. I slowly came to the realization that others were not responsible for the condition and direction of my life.

When I could acknowledge the places within me that were awake and act from that place of awareness, I began to see those aspects of my life in which I was still asleep.

When I became sexually active as a young woman, I knew that this choice came with a great deal of responsibility. I wanted to make sure that I would not get pregnant, so I used the most effective means I knew of at that time: birth control pills. I was already beginning to explore consciousness and spirituality, and as I considered my possibilities, I saw that if I was truly committed to a path of mastery, I would have to own that a master knows he or she is at choice in each moment. What power there was for me in knowing that! It followed that if I was committed to such a path, then I was also at choice as to whether or not I would conceive each time I had sex. So I stopped taking the pill, with all its side effects, and began to use a new form of inner birth control that was inspired by my choice to have mastery over my female biology. I called it psychic birth control.

During my college years, the women's movement became a strong force in this country. It made me keenly aware of the inequities between the sexes in our culture. A lot of anger and bitterness surrounded these issues, and for all the talk of consciousness-raising, the movement was basically a political and cultural phenomenon. However, when I began to pursue a spiritual path, I learned that if I was in my authentic power, others were not responsible for the condition and direction of my life.

What I chose and what happened to me as a consequence were entirely up to me.

So much historical and cultural information about the victimization of women by men, was made available at that time, and it felt important for me to not buy into it or feed it. That decision in turn, reinforced my commitment to psychic birth control. Perhaps that commitment was also informed by former lifetimes, of having babies I did not want and felt forced to have. In any case, it felt like an important personal mission to have mastery over my body in this way.

This reminds me of an experiment I learned about in sociology class in which two sets of kittens were raised in different environments. One environment had only horizontal lines, the other environment only vertical ones. When the cats were released into a natural environment, those that were raised with horizontal lines would bump into the legs of chairs because they could not perceive the vertical lines of the chairs. The cats raised in the vertical environment could not jump up on the couch because they could not see horizontal lines.

Most women are like those kittens, seeing and believing that every time they have sex, they are in danger of getting pregnant. I was no longer willing to be constrained by the belief and perception that having sex meant I might get pregnant and that I was a victim of a man's semen. This was truly a woman's liberation! Since I knew I did not want to have children, I simply commanded my body to not conceive. This was also very sexually freeing for the man.

After practicing this form of birth control successfully for five years, I offered a class to women called *Mastery of Conception*. Curiously, each time I offered the class, only a handful of women signed up. When I questioned other women about possibly learning this empowering technique, many of them responded that they were not interested in having that kind of power. The amazing thing is that twenty-five years later, I still hear from many of the graduates of those early workshops, and the one thing they all share is how being empowered in this part of their lives carried over into many other areas. The trust they had that each month their period would arrive gave them a peace of mind that a pill or device could never give. They acknowledged that the day they learned psychic birth control was the day they switched from fear-based sexuality to a relaxed and empowered sexuality.

I have such compassion for the woman who sits in front of me and, facing an unwanted pregnancy, looks up and says, "I just *look* at a man and I get pregnant." I think, How sad, because I realize how much fear and conditioning goes with her to the bed each time she has sex.

This type of mastery indicates some important characteristics of owning one's power that should be kept in mind:

- Remaining present in the body

- Refusing to be victimized by anything or anyone

- Not excluding the other—in this case, the man

Authentic power includes everyone. We may have differing viewpoints, but the other is not to be thrown out of your heart.

So with psychic birth control as the metaphor, one wonders, What makes one person gravitate to a process that would empower their life, while another runs in the opposite direction? In our work with people over the years, we have seen that people tend to handicap themselves when it comes to power. For instance, just because I created mastery with my reproductive organs doesn't mean that I am fully empowered in every aspect of my life. Sit me down in front of a banker or mortgage broker to negotiate a loan, and I become easily confused.

As I discussed earlier, I began to handicap myself at the age of nine concerning money. After losing my leg, I was faced with the responsibility of handling a large sum of money from the lawsuit, as well as the implicit power that money brought. It was too much for a little girl to deal with, and the trauma of it carried over into my adult life.

Daniel

A man came to see me who was feeling frustrated and dissatisfied with his life. He recounted several incidents, and the one thing they had in common was that, in each situation, he held back from expressing his contrary views to others. He would *think* about how he disagreed, but he would rarely *state* his objections. When I pointed out to him his reluctance to speak up, he expressed the confusion I see in so many people who are afraid to own their power. When I pressed him on his reluctance, he simply said, "I don't want to appear egotistical."

Summoning the courage to assert our feelings and views is like developing a muscle in the body; it needs exercise and practice to become useful and effective. Initially we may not have the exact words, but being willing to move into that socially awkward space by perhaps saying, "Something here doesn't feel quite right to me" is the first step. Fear and anxiety may well be present at times like these, but speaking and acting in spite of our fear is what courage is all about.

As we have reminded many clients who feel like they're between a rock and a hard place, "I'd rather be hated for who I am than loved for who I am not."

Angela

Angela was a thirty-seven-year-old woman whose voice made her sound like a sixteen-year-old Valley girl. To my ears, it was like chalk on a blackboard. When I would talk to her in a direct manner, she would often meet me with a very different voice, one that carried some authority and power. Yet she could not sustain it and would revert to talking like a flighty teenager, her head bobbing from side to side. I clearly had my work cut out for me. I pointed out to her how her voice would change according to the circumstances and I explained the mixed message she was broadcasting to the world about herself. She became defensive and accused me of being confrontive (sometimes the truth *is* confrontive!), insisting that power could be gentle. When we explored her background it became clear that as a little girl she'd longed for, but never really felt, the love and approval of her father. As a result she was still quite stuck in her childhood, especially in the ways she related to men. Not having developed the courage to assert her desires in a womanly way, she resorted to her teenage feminine wiles, relying on flirting and sexual manipulation with the men in her life.

Angela was convinced that I was judging her, and after our second session, she didn't come back. This sometimes happens, but in the majority of those cases, I hear from the person again, often as much as a year or two later. Invariably, they acknowledge the truth of what I said at the time, and admit that their ego couldn't let it in. I hope that Angela calls me again—and she may not. I respect her choice either way.

On a subconscious level, many of us still want to remain children. Sometimes it is because of a longing for the love and approval of a parent and sometimes it's simply not wanting to grow up.

The degree to which we are stuck in our childhood is the degree to which we are not in our power.

Lorretta

When Lorretta was sexually abused by a friend of the family at the age of five, she tried to tell her mother about it. Lorretta loved her mother and actually had her on a pedestal. When her mother refused to believe her, Lorretta buried inside what happened to her and made a life-altering decision that plagued her for the next fifty years: "The people I love don't listen to me, so why bother speaking up for myself?"

As an impressionable little girl, she had begun the process of handicapping herself and her power in the way many of us do it: through feelings of resignation and an underlying belief that we are not deserving. This prevents us from fully being in our power and expressing that power in the world.

Although the handicapping begins early in life, it often doesn't show up until we take on a new challenge, such as a love relationship. We may enter it with a clear idea of how we want to be treated, seen, honored and respected, but somewhere along the line, we find ourselves going along with something that isn't in accordance with our highest good. Yet again, we've let ourselves be controlled by those old decisions and beliefs about unworthiness and we become resigned and give up.

Many people have handicapped their power through religious beliefs and spiritual vows from past lives. They may even see spirituality and power as mutually exclusive. This shows how much confusion exists regarding the true nature of power. It is thought to have something to do with control and forcing our will on others. The ability to control and manipulate is certainly effective in achieving a type of outward power that is envied by others. But of course, whenever someone's success is based on pain and separation, the karmic wheel is set in motion, and sooner or later, a price is paid for that type of activity.

Well-intentioned people happily give up the pursuit of money and power, hoping that will further their spiritual growth and contribute to a better world. Ironically, the world will only undergo a spiritual transformation when Lightworkers finally accept the challenge of owning their own power and expressing it in the world in a healthy way, no longer leaving the destiny of the world in the hands of the misguided and greedy.

Authentic power is action informed by our heart and our soul. It is participation in the world of activity but from a higher perspective, one that is in harmony with one's inner truth and principles and less concerned with the outer indicators of success and failure.

Thus, Mahatma Gandhi, a ninety-pound Indian, standing for the principle of the intrinsic dignity of man and his right to freedom, virtually single-handedly overcame the British Empire, then the greatest force in the world.

To heal the fear of owning our power, we must put ourselves in situations that take us out of our comfort zone and challenge us to risk and to respond spontaneously, rather than relying on the safe and predictable. Some people like to challenge themselves with athletic endeavors, but this usually doesn't touch the ways we're wounded in our relations with others.

Many years ago, Hugh attended a weekend workshop, and immediately noticed a woman who was shy and reticent. She was barely participating, and when she spoke, it was in a wispy, girlish voice—and this was a woman in her early thirties. On the final day, during a strenuous group exercise, Hugh swung around and accidentally smacked this woman full in the face with the back of his hand. She fell to the floor, and looking totally shocked, sat there, stunned, for a full minute. Suddenly, she started to laugh heartily, a real belly laugh that shook her whole body. Everyone looked on in amazement as this shrinking violet was transformed into a vibrant, juicy woman. Even her skin changed, becoming pink and glowing. When she was finally able to speak, she explained that her biggest fear in coming to this workshop was the possibility of a physical confrontation of some kind. She said, "I was shocked that when he hit me, it didn't really hurt in a way that I feared it might—it just felt all tingly. And now I feel totally alive."

By gathering the courage to put herself in a situation that would challenge her, she created a great lesson for herself.

Our decisions and actions ripple through the universe of consciousness to affect the lives of all. As the new physics has shown, everything in the universe is connected with everything else. Even seemingly random and accidental events can carry great significance and lessons, as illustrated by the above anecdote.

To reclaim our power and vitality, we may need to give ourselves opportunities for "accidents" and experiences such as this. Be open to the mystery and magic of life. As the song by John Lennon so aptly put it, "Life is what happens while we're busy making other plans."

EXERCISE
Understanding the Role of Power in Your Life

This is a writing exercise. It's important to ask yourself some pertinent questions so you can begin to understand your relationship to your own power.

• How do you define "being in your power"?

• What drains your power?

• Do you feel as if people have power over you? Describe this in more detail.

• Does an incident from your past still have the power to make you feel less about yourself? If yes, what is it? Be specific. How does this incident make you feel less about yourself?

• Do you find yourself empowered when you are with one group of people and disempowered around other groups? Write about this in detail.

• Are you afraid to be your true self? If yes, why?

• Are there ways you handicap yourself? If yes, explain in detail your style of handicapping yourself.

RELEASING PROCESS

- I release, from my gut, all the words I've swallowed instead of expressing my power.

- I release my fear of fully owning and expressing my power.

- I release all the acids and toxins running through my spleen, pancreas, stomach, and liver that came from my confusion between control and power.

- I release from my *third chakra all the inappropriate ways I feel I need to be responsible for others.

- I release all unforgiveness of myself for all those times, in this lifetime and others, when I misused my power and hurt others.

- I release the effects of others abusing me with their power.

- I release convincing myself that I am a victim, powerless and ineffective at doing anything about it. No more!

- I release all my confusion between authentic power and power generated from my personality.

- I release my decision to not use my power in this lifetime because of how I misused my power in other lifetimes.

- I release punishing myself for that lifetime by not owning my power in this one.

- I release all unforgiveness toward myself for all those I hurt through my misuse of power, and I invite them to be with me now to balance out all misqualified energies.

- I ask forgiveness and I forgive myself.

- It is safe for me now to own and use my power. I make a new decision to step into my power center and claim it totally and completely.

*inner power center located at the solar plexus

12

Hindrance #5:
Lack of Impeccability

Aim above morality. Be not simply good; be good for something.

—Henry David Thoreau

We are using the word "impeccable" here to define a way of being in the world to which all humans must aspire if they are going to evolve beyond the imposed morality of their culture. We define impeccability as "living from the highest level of Light that you have achieved."

Impeccability is not about feeling superior or aloof, but simply realizing that there is a personal, inner chord of truth to which we must attune ourselves rather than simply following the outer rules of society. A person follows those rules and laws because they fear punishment, either from the courts or a vengeful God. But as you evolve and grow in consciousness, you begin to establish your own personal honor code by which you live. This code comes not from your family or Sunday school but from your own inner guidance. Even the words "right" and "wrong" become too primitive and simplistic. Every life situation is unique and requires us to act spontaneously, instead of from commandments written in stone. When you're impeccable, you act from your gut and your heart, in a way that is appropriate to the situation. It has less to do with keeping your word to someone else and everything to do with keeping your word to yourself.

When a person first breaks away from their culture, they often get stuck in a rebellious stance, acting out with anti-social behavior, perhaps even breaking laws and calling it freedom. This is an immature form of freedom achieved by reacting against society and seeking the transitory pleasures of the moment. An intelligent person doesn't stay in this phase for very long.

A whole body of literature exists about the path of the outsider, ranging from *Jonathan Livingston Seagull* to works by Albert Camus. These books explore the individual's transition from being attached to a kind of security in the "warmth of the herd" to acting impeccably and pursuing one's Higher Truth.

With the freedom of being an autonomous individual comes the responsibility to act impeccably. In fact, when you aren't acting impeccably, you're not being congruent with your heart and your truth. The fallout from this incongruency eventually shows up as tension or conflict in your life. Somewhere in your consciousness, you keep ducking your head, wondering how and when the fallout is going to appear. This very act of ducking actually causes self-punishment and a belief that you don't deserve to have what you want. In fact, guilt caused by not being impeccable can dominate one's life.

When you take action that is in opposition to what you know in your heart to be true, it creates leaks in your energy field, thus creating a breakdown in the strength and integrity of your energetic and physical form. This results in sickness, disease and/or a breakdown in your relationships.

In the movie *Scent of a Woman*, Al Pacino, in an Oscar-winning performance, makes a speech in defense of a young man named Charlie, who is about to take responsibility for something that his fellow students from so-called proper backgrounds are hoping to get away with. Pacino's character acknowledges that he hasn't acted impeccably in his own life and took an easier road instead. The cumulative effect of this way of living caused him to lose his eyesight. He admires and respects Charlie, "because to choose the right road is much harder."

To know what the right road is for us, we must ask ourselves, "What will it take for me to be impeccable?" and then courageously take the appropriate action. This may mean eliminating any rationalizations that get you off the hook, that excuse your lack of impeccability. In simple terms this means walking your talk.

The following case studies and exercises will assist you in developing your impeccability.

Lucy

Lucy's story reveals the disparity between *believing* that we're impeccable and actually *acting* impeccably.

Lucy participated in one of our Releasing Intensives. She was clearly in a lot of psychic pain, some of which she was feeling, while much was beneath the surface of her awareness. Her story revealed that the family dysfunction she experienced as a child was being repeated in her own marriage and family. So we were shocked when, during the workshop, she announced, "I am more conscious then anyone here; I'm more spiritual and I know more than anyone here in this room!" I loved her for being audacious and having the courage to blurt this out. Many of us spend time in this state of mind, perhaps not saying it but certainly thinking it. I know I have. There have been times on my spiritual path when my ego wanted to claim spiritual breakthroughs as its own personal property! This kind of spiritual pride is a normal and necessary step we all have to pass through as our consciousness evolves. But I discovered later a couple of questions I could ask myself that would keep me humble and clarify when it was my ego talking. I asked Lucy these same questions that day, and I encourage you to answer them now for yourself.

Remember to check back with your list of your heart's desires to see if a lack of impeccability is hindering you from reaching them.

EXERCISE
Walking Your Talk

A. To get the most out of this exercise, you must be willing to be a little playful. For a few minutes, we'd like you to be like Lucy. Get up on your high horse and brag about all the ways you are more spiritually aware and conscious than people around you. Get in touch with that spiritual pride lurking inside you and write down five ways you feel you are spiritually evolved.

1.
2.
3.
4.
5.

B. Now, being honest and impeccable with yourself, list all the ways that each of these truths is demonstrated in your everyday life. How do they show up in your relating with others?

1.
2.
3.
4.
5.

If it's difficult to describe how these truths are demonstrated in your life, it may mean that in some ways, you are not walking your talk.

The point of this exercise is to understand that it doesn't matter what you know spiritually if it isn't showing up in your life. In other words, spiritual knowledge is just that—knowledge. It's not worth a thing if it's not integrated into your everyday life.

An incident from the life of Ramakrishna, a great Indian mystic, illustrates this point. He was constantly encouraging people to incorporate their spiritual practice into their everyday, domestic life instead of wandering off to a cave to meditate. One day, he was about to cross a river on a ferry boat when someone called his name. It was a yogi walking on the surface of the river. He shouted, "Ramakrishna! If you are such a great saint, why don't you join me and walk across the water?"

Ramakrishna turned to the boatman and asked him what the fee was to take the ferry. "One rupee," came the response. Ramakrishna then asked the yogi, "How long did it take you to learn to walk on water?"

With all of his spiritual pride showing, the yogi responded, "seventeen years of deep meditation and austerities."

Ramkrishna then said to him, "As I see it, you have taken seventeen years to develop a skill that is worth only one rupee. What a waste of time and energy!"

So even if you do go beyond spiritual knowledge and develop spiritual *siddhis*, or powers, if they don't have a beneficial effect on your life or serve others, they have no true intrinsic value.

Sam

Sam's case illustrates how lack of impeccability keeps us feeling guilty and undeserving of our heart's desires.

Sam came to me for private sessions after a three-year relationship ended badly. He hated his job, but even though he had saved a large nest egg and could afford a two-year sabbatical, for some reason he felt he should stay with this mind-numbing job. He was forty-five and, as he put it, "I don't know what I want to be when I grow up." He seemed powerless to make good decisions for himself.

After several sessions, much was revealed about decisions he had made about himself growing up that now comprised his inner makeup. One by one, his dreams had fallen through the cracks. Even though he was a straight-A student and could have gotten a scholarship, his father told him there was no way Sam could afford to go to that Ivy League college. When he did finally graduate from a city college, he wanted to work in the family business, but his father told him his brother had already filled the position. Even a VW Bug he wanted was denied him because his mother felt it was an unsafe car, so his father arranged for a safer model. Sam began to live in resignation and stopped making decisions for himself, letting happenstance rule his life.

The final piece came during a session when he was releasing his confusion around what it is to really be a man. As he released, tears filled his eyes as a memory came bubbling to the surface.

It was the memory of his high school girlfriend becoming pregnant with his child, and his not hearing about it until weeks before the birth. The whole thing was handled with Sam totally excluded. The girl didn't want to tell him because she knew how much college meant to him and didn't want the pregnancy to ruin it for him. So one afternoon, his parents met with the girl's, some money was exchanged, and Sam wasn't "inconvenienced by this little mess." From that point on, he never had to take responsibility or be accountable for his part in the situation in any way. Sadly, this crippled him in the taking responsibility department.

Sam has been caught in the dichotomy of feeling tremendous guilt and shame about his lack of impeccability in "not doing right by the girl" and keeping the perks his silence brought him by dodging his accountability. He didn't know what he wanted to be when he grew up because he had never been able to make a grown-up decision for himself. He didn't have any experiences of staying committed in the face of difficulties in order to achieve a desired outcome. This process of responsible decision-making and follow-through is the foundation for creating our heart's desires; and it is something we all have to learn in order to truly grow up.

Does Sam's story resonate in any way with your own life? Have there been times when you rode on your family's shirttails to get you through an awkward situation? Have you dodged responsibility by not stepping up to the plate and accepting the consequences of your actions? Do you notice a disparity between your spiritual beliefs and the way your life is unfolding?

If you answer yes to any of these questions, then there is a lack of impeccability in your life that is a hindrance to your creating your heart's desires. The following exercises and Releasing will help you heal this pattern.

EXERCISE
Becoming Impeccable and Increasing Your Acceptance Level

To receive your heart's desires, you must have a sufficient acceptance level. What you can accept, what you let yourself have, is directly related to how impeccable you feel in your life. So the first thing to look at are the ways you aren't being impeccable.

- Using the following chart, observe your life, past and present, and make a list of any ways that you're not being impeccable. Consider family matters, relationships, money, career, and your inner or spiritual world.

- For each item, write what it will take for you to correct or realign your behavior so that it will be impeccable. Perhaps something needs to be communicated, paid for, forgiven, (yourself or others) and released.

- When will you complete each item so you can feel impeccable? Perhaps set a deadline, making sure that it is reasonable but doesn't give you too much slack.

When you feel impeccable, you will feel worthy to receive.

We realize that this exercise can be a major task and may take months to complete. It might be easier if you start with the least challenging item. Be gentle with yourself and others.

Becoming Impeccable

Ways I'm Not Impeccable	How Can I Be Impeccable?	When Will It Be Done?

RELEASING PROCESS

Here are the Releasing statements pertaining to Sam's story. You are encouraged to repeat them for yourself and then create your own Releasing statements regarding your past. And again, allow up any emotions that are stirred.

- I release my confusion from the inherited programming from my parents that "men (women) get away with things."

- I release my rage and anger toward my parents for not encouraging me to make my own decisions.

- I release my guilt and sadness for not speaking up when I heard about the pregnancy (or fill in your own incident).

- I release all unforgiveness toward myself for not rising to the occasion.

- I release my fear of any conflict that results from my acting impeccably.

- I release the inherited family programming that says, "It's better to be safe and secure than to take any risks in life."

- I release my fear of failure and rejection in going for what makes my heart sing.

- I release my fear of actually receiving what makes my heart sing.

- I release my soul pattern and tendency to let other people make decisions for my life and then resent them for it later.

- I release my unwillingness to make decisions for my life.

- I release my fear of facing the consequences of my decisions, knowing I'll have no one else to blame for them except myself.

- I ask the God within to transmute all those soul aspects into the Light to neutralize all cell memory and output from them that have been invested in this pattern for so long. No more!

- I choose now to call my Spirit back from all those times in the past when others made decisions for me. I ask the God within to reconnect with me now the part of my Spirit that broke off and bring it into present time.

- I choose now to call my power back from all those people to whom I gave my power.

- I choose now to own my power and I choose to step into my third chakra totally and completely and start today to make decisions for my life. As uncomfortable as that may be for me now, I choose to do this.

13

Hindrance #6:
Unwillingness to Forgive

A grievance needs to be recreated daily in order for it exist.

Forgiveness is certainly one of the most challenging lessons on this planet, and I have had my share of difficulties with it in my life. Some people and situations have been fairly easy to forgive, while with others, it has seemed almost impossible. When it felt impossible, it was because I'd forgotten that the process of forgiveness was more for my benefit than for others. The error lay in shifting my focus from my own inner experience to becoming preoccupied with the injustice I believed had been done to me by that person. Fueled by my anger, I would be off and running, justifying all the reasons why I would never forgive someone. Behaving this way, I unwittingly enrolled myself in recreating the grievance against that person from then on, for years to come.

Is there someone in your life whom you feel you can never forgive? It's important for you to understand how this feeling affects you. Examining it closely, you will see that holding on to this grievance has a debilitating effect on your body, mind, and spirit. And whether you are conscious of it or not, every day when you wake up, a part of you is choosing to recreate that grievance to keep it alive. It's just like putting a heavy chip on your shoulder every morning that weighs you down and consumes your energy. The grievance does not have a life of its own; it needs to be recreated every day, moment to moment, in order for it to exist. And the more people you keep on your unforgiveness list, the more you deplete your life energy.

Why is it so difficult for us to simply let go, forgive, and move on? We cling to past grievances, resentments and painful memories, hanging on years after the episode occurred. We become fixated on a desire for justice, or even revenge, to be meted out to the perpetrator, imagining this will give us some satisfaction. We long for human justice; we demand that the situation be resolved the way *we* want it, instead of turning it over to God and a higher form of resolution and peace. We become overly identified with our side of the story, and get stuck in our hurt, our pride, our indignation. The truth is that somewhere inside us, we know that by the very act of forgiveness, our life will change drastically, and yet we are afraid of such a change. If you reflect on it, there is no one whose life has changed for the worse because they forgave someone.

Take a moment and remember a time you were physically hurt as a child. Perhaps you fell off the swing, or skinned your knee running to first base, or even more dramatically, you broke your leg or arm. As you remember the incident, does that body part still hurt you today? Probably not, because the resilience of the physical body allows those wounds to heal rather rapidly. Just as our physical bodies were never meant to still hurt after a fall that happened twenty years ago, we were not meant to continue suffering from an emotional wound that happened twenty years ago.

To keep the emotional pain alive from something that someone said or did a long time ago, on some level of our being we must choose each day to recreate that wound, that attack, in order for it to still exist in our life. So each morning, you are waking up and sending vital life force energy back into a past event and asking to be hurt all over again. This is one way we disempower ourselves and drain our own vitality. The immune system cannot handle this and in time, the physical body starts to hurt and even becomes diseased.

If the effect of the unforgiveness isn't showing up in the physical body, then it will show up in relationship problems or even financial setbacks. It all depends on how you were wired to learn. Some people receive their wake-up call through painful life events such as not being able to pay their MasterCard bill, being fired from a job, or a relationship falling apart. However, if anger and resentment festers inside long enough, it is bound to show up as a physical ailment. The affected part of the body and type of sickness is directly related to the type of betrayal or offense committed. For example, betrayal in love may result in heart-related disease, and unresolved anger and forgiveness can result in liver disease.

C.G. Jung said, "The Gods visit us through illness."

I do not mean to undermine or invalidate the impact of a truly traumatic event from anyone's past. Some horrific things happened in my childhood from which I thought I would never recover. And you can always find much social agreement for your "right" to hold on to unforgiveness from being wronged as a child.

Forgiveness of childhood abuses is a long-term process. I did not wake up one day and say to myself, "I am now going to forgive my father for driving drunk and contributing to the accident in which I lost my leg. And while I'm at it, I'll also forgive my mother for not knowing how to mother me." That is not how authentic forgiveness comes about. I first had to go through the process of *feeling* the enormity of that pain, having someone witness my pain and then releasing the effects of those traumatic events that were still living inside of me and creating havoc in my outer world. I could then move on to forgiveness. One of the benefits of coming through to the other side is that I could then view my life from a higher perspective. I no longer took the events surrounding the accident so personally and I could see from a soul level what I was to learn by being in a physical body with one leg.

Similarly, when we experience an injustice or a betrayal in present time, it's normal and healthy to feel a range of uncomfortable emotions—from rage and anger to sadness and grief. Any kind of premature forgiveness or "turning the other cheek" rips us off from a spontaneous expression of healthy emotion. After this initial reaction has run its course, we can then move into the process of forgiveness.

Jesse

Jesse arrived for a session and promptly told me he was so depressed that he was considering two options: go on Prozac, and if that didn't work, commit suicide. When he shared these options with a close friend who happened to be a client of mine, she suggested, "Jesse, before trying Prozac or suicide, go and see Voge."

As the session began, Jesse wasn't at all forthcoming. I could see that he was going to put up a good fight before he would give up the idea of taking Prozac. Fifteen minutes into the session, I silently said a little prayer: "Spirit, I don't think I can help him. Either he does not want the help at this time or I just don't see how I can get in and connect with him, so if you want me to help him, please show me the way or I'll have to ask him to leave." In the next moment, he began to open up, telling me about the ways he was not nurtured as a child by his mother and his inability to forgive her. He acknowledged that he felt very stuck in this depressed state, believing he would never be truly seen by loved ones in his life. I shared with him a story that had been offered to me many years before. It was pivotal in moving me forward on my journey to the forgiveness of my mother.

This image has been very valuable for many of my clients when they've run up against a tough customer that is difficult to forgive. So we encourage you to immerse yourself in the story as much as possible to receive the maximum benefit.

- Imagine that an old friend you haven't seen in a long time calls and tells you they are here on business and have a short time to visit. This person is very dear to your heart, so of course you cancel all your plans and invite your friend to come over for dinner. That afternoon, you run around, shopping for everything you need. You go to the wine store for that perfect chardonnay, then to the florist for a beautiful arrangement. Suddenly, you remember that the clothes you wanted to wear are still in the cleaners. Arms loaded with all that's needed for a great evening, you rush over to the cleaners, and someone who is not looking where they are going crashes into you and sends the flowers flying, and the groceries bouncing.

- Imagine how you feel toward this person for not looking where they were going.
- Really let yourself feel it.
- What are the first words that want to come out of your mouth?
- On a scale of 1 to 10, notice how angry you are.
- Now take a breath and look down at the ground where the flowers and groceries are scattered. You notice the tip of a white cane. Follow the cane up to the person's hand, and then lift your gaze up to his eyes. The person in front of you is blind. He isn't unconscious, stupid or malicious, just blind.
- Now how do you feel toward this person?
- On a scale of 1 to 10, how angry are you?

Sometimes the person we believe has hurt us the most is also blind and is simply acting out of their blindness. Sometimes we are the one who is acting out of *our* blindness toward another.

- Close your eyes and again imagine the above story with every vivid detail.

- When you get to the blind person, imagine the face of whoever has hurt you the most. Choose the person you are having the most difficult time forgiving, the person with whom you are choosing to recreate a grievance every day of your life—sending your energy back in time when it's truly needed to nurture you in present time.

- See that person not as your enemy but as blind and acting out of their blindness.

- From this different perspective, can you forgive them for the actions that came out of their blindness?

- Talk to the soul of that person saying, "(Their name), I want to talk to you on the soul level. When this happened to me, I felt_____."

- Continue talking to them from this new awareness of their blindness until you can look into their eyes and forgive them, not from your mind, but from your heart.

- Finally, there is one more person for you to see as blind and who deserves your forgiveness: you.

When I took Jesse through this process, he broke down and sobbed like a baby. All those years, he had believed there was something wrong with *him* that made his mother act so cruelly and unloving. When he saw his mother as blind, a heaviness and despair that had been with him for years subsided and he could accept himself for who he was. Crying tears of relief, he said, "I can forgive my mother now, finally." Jesse didn't go on Prozac, and he is still on the planet, enjoying his life more than ever.

A recent poll of attorneys revealed that thirty-seven percent of all litigation could have been prevented by an apology. Of course, when we are acting out of our blindness, we see no reason to apologize. Our self-righteous anger always feels justified.

Years ago, when Hugh and I were still renters, we had a major confrontation with our landlord. It continued to escalate until legal action seemed inevitable. Both we and the landlord were stuck in our positions and unwilling to budge. In our frustration, we turned to our dear friend Lew Epstein to get his take on the situation. Lew had many years of experience in leading seminars in the human potential movement. After we told him our story, he asked, "Is there anything else?"

"No, Lewie, that's the whole story," I replied. We were now prepared to hear Lew say how right we were and that the landlord should rot in hell for everything he was putting us through. But his advice was the last thing we expected to hear. He said, "You need to call your landlord and apologize to him." We could not believe our ears. His suggestion was a slightly different version of Waduda's advice to me: that it is the responsibility of the more conscious person to resolve the situation. Lew showed us how we were perpetuating the grievance and intensifying the drama. Our apology to the landlord defused the situation and paved the way for a compromise that suited all concerned.

Truly forgiving those who have hurt us is not possible in any meaningful way until we have fully felt our genuine emotions regarding a given situation—and those emotions have often been buried for years. Forgiveness comes only after we have felt our pain completely. We come to it in our own time and wisdom. Once the emotional pain of the past is felt and released, our inner reality begins to change and, partly through grace, forgiveness becomes a possibility.

EXERCISE
Identifying a Grievance and Speaking It Out Loud

- Close your eyes and ask Spirit to show you which illnesses or painful life events can be traced to a long-held grievance.

- Having identified a grievance, find someone you trust to witness all the pain you still have around it. This may be a trusted friend or a therapist who will listen with an open heart and without any judgment. It is important that they simply listen to you and not try to fix you or the situation, or invalidate what you are feeling.

  In one of our six-month trainings, a woman named Kate broke down with a lot of emotion she had been holding since childhood. As soon as she started to cry, another woman went over to comfort her, and Kate's tears began to subside. On the surface, this looks like the compassionate thing to do, so the woman was shocked when I became angry and told her to immediately move away from Kate. I said to her, "It's taken Kate six months to finally get in touch with her feelings, and in just thirty seconds, you've ripped her off of the experience. Her emotions make you uncomfortable, and your ego is convincing you that you have the power to make her feel better." To her credit, she understood and moved away, which allowed Kate to reconnect with her emotions until they fully drained and we could then move on to releasing. Be wary of well-intentioned friends who want to make it all better for you. Their caretaking may feel great in the moment, but it might be short-circuiting a very natural healing process.

- Speaking your grievance aloud and allowing yourself to feel the emotions around it, opens you up to the Light of grace descending to change the energy of that grievance into forgiveness.

RELEASING PROCESS

- I release my fear of letting go of this grievance.

- I release my belief that I need this grievance in order to feel powerful.

- I release my insistence on justice, payback, and revenge.

- I release my investment in getting sympathy for being the victim.

- I release the habit of recreating this grievance every day.

- I release the layers upon layers of resentment that have built up in my physical body from holding on to this grievance.

- I release the harmful effects of that resentment, including the tension and toxins stored in my physical body.

- I release my shock and sadness at realizing how holding this grievance has harmed my body, mind, and spirit.

- I release from my gallbladder all that has galled me.

- I release from my liver all the anger from holding on to this grievance. I ask the God within to transmute it now.

- I release all unforgiveness toward (their name) for (the event).

- I release my fear of creating something new for myself each day.

- I choose now to forgive myself totally and completely.

- I make a new decision to turn justice over to God.

14

Hindrance #7:
Fear of the Light

To become our best, we must first face our worst.

For many of us, the dark side is an elusive energy cloaked in mystery. It is loaded with our old Sunday school programming about the devil and childhood fears evoked by things that go bump in the night. We learned to avoid and run from those dark forces, never wondering or considering how we ourselves fit in to this mystery. However, in spite of what we've been taught, and as daunting a task as it seems, in order for us to reach our full potential and step fully into the Light, it is necessary that we turn and face our own darkness. As the quotation above states: To become our best, we must first face our worst.

Like so many men who came home from World War II, my father returned from the war a broken man in many ways. Our family was often awakened in the middle of the night by his shouts and moans, tormented as he was in his nightmares of war. Those nightmares continued until the day he died. He was a haunted man: haunted by the devastation of war, of losing his buddies, and haunted by the souls of those he had killed in combat. His inability to digest and process all these highly charged memories kept him haunted, and like so many, he resorted to alcohol to self-medicate his pain.

A friend named Alice whom I've known since childhood has had a long-term drinking problem that I watched as it continued to progress over time. If years passed without seeing each other, we would exchange pictures in our Christmas cards. Like so many alcoholics, she had the uncanny ability to hide this problem from those close to her, but I would think aloud when I saw her face, "Ah, Alice is still drinking heavily." When I looked at these photos, it wasn't so much her aging I saw; what I was seeing was the presence of another energy that was running the show and keeping Alice in cabernet.

These two stories illustrate how dark energies or forces can run a person's life. Our culture even alludes to this phenomenon through figures of speech such as "being haunted," "having a monkey on her back," and "the devil made me do it." But these phrases are such a part of our vernacular that very little consideration is given to what is truly going on under the surface. Even if one hasn't been involved in something as life-altering as war or alcoholism, each of us is susceptible to energies we are not always conscious of or cannot see.

All cultures and civilizations have acknowledged the presence of malevolent as well as benevolent spirits. The actions of spirits have been recorded in the Torah of Judaism, the New Testament of Christianity, and the Koran of Islam. Anthropologists have for decades recorded the relationship between indigenous cultures and the spirit realm.

In our increasingly secular world, it is important that we not overlook the influence of the old myths and metaphors of ancient times simply because we don't relate to them. Perhaps through some updated metaphors and examples, we can grasp the significance of the spirit realm in our lives, thus empowering us and furthering our inner journey toward wholeness and the Light.

The human soul has a lower self and a Higher Self. Our lower self is motivated by our more primitive instincts and emotions, such as fear and greed. Our Higher Self aspires to more refined ways of being such as compassion, joy, and love. Moving beyond the activities of the lower self and evolving into the Higher Self is, in a nutshell, what being on this planet is all about. Of course, it is a profound challenge, and how we deal with the influence of spiritual entities is one of the tests.

The physical realm is such a desirable place to be that whenever a human being is present, Spirit beings of varying degrees of consciousness are always nearby. Some of these higher and helpful Spirit entities are called angels or guides, while the potentially harmful entities are seen as implants or parasitic energies. Hugh and I call the latter barnacles. As humans, we all have our flaws, our shortcomings, our ways of handing the reins over to our lower self, our lower nature. It is when we gratify these lower desires in an unconscious way that we open ourselves to a barnacle latching on and coming along for the ride. For example if you love chocolates, and you over indulge, be assured that there is a "chocolate barnacle" attaching on to you and getting vicarious pleasure through your habit of sweets. You may even find yourself looking at an empty box of chocolates one day, shocked at how you could have eaten them all so quickly and so unconsciously. This is because you had a little help from a barnacle.

The more we indulge in the habits and tendencies of our lower self, the more we attract different types of barnacles that literally feed off of these base human energies. Fear, shame, guilt, lust, and jealousy are all "bait" for barnacles. For example, if you are prone to sudden outbursts of anger, then you may have a barnacle that is attracted to this energy. Your indulgence in anger is an invitation for the barnacle to come and feed. It is through flaws such as these that barnacles attach onto us, weighing us down and slowing our spiritual growth and evolution.

What we are describing is really no different from how the physical world operates. During my college days, I found myself in a circle of friends that bonded primarily through gossip. I found myself enjoying the stories and scandals, without questioning whether or not they were true. Then one day, I found myself the object of my friends' gossip, and I was terribly hurt. It was a wake-up call for me because I realized that through wanting to be accepted by these girls, I was attracting that hurtful energy toward me. I vowed to be more mindful of this behavior, and slowly I noticed that when I stopped engaging in their rumor mill, I was invited less and less often to be one of the gang. Those friendships just fell away one by one. Soon I found friends who knew how to be close in kinder, more loving ways, without needing to diminish others.

This dynamic pertains to the spirit barnacles as well. The more we choose to gratify our base desires, and the less aware we are of the negative effects, the stronger the influence of the barnacle and the tighter its grip. Conversely, the less we give in to our lower energies, the less we attract these barnacles to us. So to protect ourselves against these influences, we must honestly face our flaws and what they attract.

In discussing barnacles with our clients, a question that often comes up is, "If there are both harmful and beneficial Spirit entities, why don't we simply focus on the more evolved entities?" The main reason is that we simply have forgotten that the purpose in our being on the planet is to learn how to move into the Light and serve others in doing the same. This forgetfulness, of course, takes many forms, ranging from self-pity to self-importance, but they all boil down to forgetting our true divine nature. This form of amnesia is reinforced by the barnacles. They have a vested interest in humans remaining ensnared in the darkness.

As a little boy around the age of nine or ten, Hugh had a tough time with insomnia and dark-side monsters that invaded his bedroom. This went on for months until one night he was able to stare the demons down and watch in amazement as they retreated. In the morning, he felt a new sense of peace and a realization that everything was going to be fine. Wanting to hang on to this newfound gift, he wrote on each month of his bedside calendar the word "Remember." This helped him for a while, but with the onset of puberty, his tenuous grasp on grace was broken once again. His raging hormones and testosterone sent him into new frontiers of chaos and insecurity. Hugh's childhood adventure illustrates very well the on-again-off-again quality of our journey toward the Light: We remember, we forget, remember, forget.

To bring back the quality of remembrance and awareness into your daily life, it is good to ask yourself, "Is it in my highest good to_____?" before making an important life decision. Then close your eyes and take a few seconds to allow your inner voice of guidance to respond.

Another reason we don't naturally invite in beneficial guidance is simply our humanity. We tend to stay with whatever feels comfortable and familiar—the warmth of the herd—even if a part of us knows full well that it isn't in our highest good. The human ego also feels threatened by change in general and by the Light in particular. Finally, we don't always recognize the difference between what is of the Light and what is a dark-side influence. It takes discernment and courage to make this important distinction.

It is important to understand that fear of the Light isn't an issue of right or wrong, good or bad. That is looking at it from a moral stance. We prefer to address the topic from the perspective of evolution and consciousness. Another way of understanding this is based on the world of physics. The more we act from our lower self, the more gross our frequency of vibration. And conversely, when we align ourselves with our Higher Self, we vibrate at higher, more refined frequencies.

But one may argue, "I meditate every day and I am committed to my growth and the truth." You must remember that if even a fraction of your consciousness has resistance to the Light, then darkness exists within. It may be something as seemingly innocuous as spiritual pride or envy, but even these traits will derail us from our movement toward the Light. Meditating on this during your quiet time, you can become conscious of exactly what influences are around you and the ways you invite them to you. As you do this, you'll be able to identify those energies that support you in your commitment to wholeness, truth, and fulfilling the will of God, and those that do not.

Dark-side entities can only affect us with our cooperation. When I willingly engaged in the gossip circle with my college friends, I was cooperating with these energies. When I did some soul-searching and acknowledged my participation and then chose something different, those barnacles as well as those friends left me. I learned two important lessons from my gossip process:

1. The pain I felt from their gossip made me aware of a flaw in me of which I'd been totally unconscious. The pain was a gift that brought my attention to a place in me that was blind, and by seeing it and taking responsibility for it, I was able to bring it into the Light.

2. Due to my insecurity and desire to be a part of the crowd, I was enjoying a false sense of power.

Any imbalance in our third chakra, our power center, is an open invitation to dark energies to attach on through our yearning or even our fear of power. Creating healthy power in one's life then becomes even more imperative. Barnacles thrive in climates where their influence can make us feel powerful or weak.

As a child, I was often overwhelmed by the darkness of two parents who drank to excess. Nights spent alone in my room, while drinking and fighting happened on the other side of the door, left me feeling powerless. My little Light often felt like a helpless opponent in the face of their darkness. In my helplessness and fear, I would sometimes wish I had someone on my side who could take care of me, a champion who could help me fight my battles against my parents. I didn't realize until years later how much that little prayer, fueled by fear and feelings of separation, opened me up to dark-side influences.

In years past, if anyone broached the subject of dark-side influences, it would send me metaphorically under the sink, quivering in the fetal position. This, of course, is just what the dark-side counts on. Although I was no longer a Catholic, my listening was still influenced by my Catholic conditioning of good versus evil, and the belief that if I had anything to do with darkness, I was bad or—even worse—evil. Facing that prospect, even as an adult, was just too scary. And so it remained a Mexican stand-off between any darkness I sensed around me and the inner darkness I had unwittingly aligned with as a child.

I hadn't realized that by not facing these inner barnacles, I was kept under their influence. As long as we are too afraid to face our own darkness, we give the dark side the power to scare us and keep us feeling diminished and powerless. For me, this didn't begin to change until a releasing session when I uttered the words, "Dark-side, all this power that you have...I'm the one who gave it to you and I am now taking my power back. You have no power here, and I now choose to step into the Light, totally and completely."

It was then that I began the journey of truly facing my darkness and collusion with the dark-side and could subsequently reclaim my own power in the Light.

Two years ago, Alice decided she'd had enough of her alcohol abuse and joined AA. Last Christmas, the snapshot she enclosed was of a very different Alice. This was a different face looking back at me—softer and more at peace. Not only was she more humble from going through the Twelve Step process, but her face was no longer haunted by the feeling of having a monkey on her back.

My father on the other hand, never was able to turn and face his demons. Like so many veterans of war, he died still tormented by his memories.

EXERCISE
Deactivating Barnacles

As human beings, we are not helpless prey to other people's negative emotions or external dark-side influences. We determine the degree to which we allow these influences in our lives. When we reject anything that does not come from the divine realm, we anchor ourselves in the Light. The less darkness those influences have to work with in us, the less power they have over us. Dark-side energies thrive on specific human foibles such as separation, confusion, and distortion. For example, the dark side feeds off of fear. So if you are full of fear, you're susceptible to any fearful energies that are around you or are directed at you.

In order to develop discernment between the Light and the dark, the first question to ask of the energy you are experiencing when you find yourself in a negative emotional state is, "Are you of the Light?"

What we have found to be true is that you will always get an answer. If the energies are of the Light, you will always get a loud yes. If the energies are not of the Light, you will either get a no or no answer. A no-answer is still an answer. In that case, call the Light to you and ask it to immediately transmute all dark-side energies into the Light. This is simply a form of conscious intention combined with prayer.

Deactivating Barnacles

If	Ask	If	If
You are in a negative emotional state,	Are you of the Light?	The answer is **Yes,** do nothing.	The answer is **No,** call the Light to you and ask it to immediately transmute all dark-side energies into the Light.

RELEASING PROCESS

- I release my belief that I do not have the power to handle these kinds of energies.

- I release my belief that I lack the courage to face the darkness.

- I release all my self-hate and disgust for absorbing these kinds of energies.

- I release all fear of these energies and of being controlled by them.

- I release all unforgiveness toward myself for turning to the dark side for power when I felt powerless.

- I release my fear of evil and the devil.

- I release convincing myself that others may be evil but I am good.

- I release convincing myself that others may be good but I am evil.

- I release my addiction to seeing everything as a good/bad polarity.

- I release my fear of being possessed or going mad.

- I ask the God within to bring to my awareness my dark side.

- I release all self-condemnation for my dark side.

- I release my tendency to overindulge in food, sugar, alcohol, etc.

- I release all self-judgment about indulgence.

- I release my fear of asking for guidance from a Higher Power.

- I ask the God within to direct me to my highest guidance.

15

Hindrance #8:
Hating the Physical

He not busy bein' born is busy dyin.'

—from the song *It's Alright Ma, I'm Only Bleeding*, by Bob Dylan

Consider these questions:

- Are you happy having a physical body?
- Do you find yourself overwhelmed being in this physical reality?
- Do you know what stops you from being comfortable in your body?
- Are you happy with your gender in this lifetime?
- Did you arrive as a girl though your parents wanted a boy, or vice versa?
- Were you ever sexually or otherwise physically abused?
- Did a parent or loved one die when you were a child?
- What do you know about the circumstances of your birth?

- Did you slide down the birth canal happy to have landed or did you struggle, laboring to get here, trying to decide if being born was a good idea or not?

- Did you feel welcomed into your new home?

- Do you ever find yourself thinking, I wish I were dead?

You may not even be aware of how this quiet little wish to return from whence you came shows up in your life.

As Dylan's lyrics imply, you're either fully exploring your potential in this world or you're engaged in leaving this world; there's no middle ground.

Take a moment now and reflect on your own life: What are *you* busy doing?

When you examine your answers to the above questions, you will see to what degree you have hate for the physical. Creating your divine love, career, or art form is tough to do if you're not fully engaged and grounded here in the physical.

Louise

Several years ago, I had a client named Louise who had just been diagnosed with breast cancer. While working with her, I saw so much resignation about leaving her physical body. In many ways, she had given up on life. During the session, I began helping her release the harmful effects that this resignation had in her life. When I had her actually say the words, "I release my hate and contempt for being in the physical body," she reacted strongly, questioning why I was having her release this.

Although only in her thirties, Louise had already twice survived breast cancer. She was still a smoker, drank to excess, indulged in recreational drugs from time to time, had many sexual partners and, not incidentally, she had been sexually abused as a child.

In other words, before her consciousness had been fully formed, before she had the time to discover for herself what it was like to fully inhabit her physical form, her father raped her, taking all of that away from her. At the age of eight, she discovered how scary it could be to inhabit a physical body. The seeds had been sown early that, for her, the physical plane is not a safe place.

It took several sessions to undo the effects of the sexual abuse as it still lived in her physical body, but she still challenged this notion that she harbored hatred for being here in the physical. "Why don't I just jump off a bridge if I hate being here so much?" she would shoot back sarcastically.

Hate for the physical is a hard thing to admit to oneself, and like most people, Louise found it easier to live in denial than face the harsh truth.

As gently as I could, I explained to her that through her current behavior: late nights in bars, smoking cigarettes, fast-food diet, and random sexual encounters, she was choosing death in the form of a slow suicide. I reminded her that she had a purpose in life, a reason for being here, and that these lifestyle choices only numbed her, preventing her from seeing the bigger picture that would take her down a different road. I told her that in spite of how she was demeaned as a child, she was worthy enough to have a purpose. This struck a deep chord within her, and she began to cry.

We have said this before, but it bears repeating. Until we see, and acknowledge, the ways we are sabotaging ourselves, we are at cross-purposes and not able to move forward with our true purpose.

Remembering that she had said she loved to write, I suggested to Louise that she keep a journal. Rather than judging herself, she was to simply record in this journal all the times during the day she said no to life as well as the times she said yes, and then see if she could discover new ways of saying yes to life! Awareness of a pattern is the key to freeing ourselves, so I knew this would be a very powerful process for her.

She followed my suggestion for several weeks and was amazed at the results. She discovered she couldn't have a cigarette without noticing that it was a function of her no to life. With each activity that normally give her instant gratification yet in the long run hurt her, she saw how she had been saying no to life over and over again. She also noticed how she'd kept herself guarded, not letting herself feel her vulnerability, fear, joy, and so many emotions that make up the richness of life.

In the ensuing months, her life began to transform because she could no longer keep repeating those life-negating patterns that she had taken for granted. Louise began to find new and creative ways to embrace life, with her yes acting as an antidote to the destructive effects of her old no. She experienced what she called more spaciousness in her days, and began naturally gravitating toward her purpose: writing. She joined a writing circle, and through her participation and their support, she began to have articles published in magazines. A year later, Louise self-published her first book of short stories.

Ellen

A woman named Ellen who attended one of our *Money Is Just the Metaphor* workshops had been diagnosed with cancer, and the prognosis was not good. We went around the room asking each participant to introduce themselves and say what they wanted from the workshop. Ellen's friend jumped in to introduce her saying, "I invited her to come because I couldn't sit back any longer and watch her die." It became very quiet in the room. All eyes went to Ellen. She spoke in a meek and defeated voice. She felt that the cancer had just happened to her, that it was much bigger than her, and that she had no power to alter the outcome of this intruder that was already ravaging her body.

As the weekend progressed, it was amazing to watch the changes in Ellen's face. Each new process brought her increased clarity and understanding concerning her relationship to money. It seems she was about to inherit a large sum of money and a lot of energy and emotion were tied up in this situation. She also saw how her family's financial programming fueled her predisposition toward cancer. With each insight, she was able to take more and more responsibility for her role in this money dance with her family. Her vitality and life force was clearly returning to her physical body as she began reclaiming the power to determine her own way with money.

From the beginning of the workshop, we had made it clear to Ellen that we would honor any intention she had to leave the physical body and that we had no judgments about this matter. Most important we reminded her that she was not a victim of this cancerous enemy, but that *the cancer was actually her chosen ally in this decision to leave the body.* To reach this perspective is difficult, but very freeing.

When the workshop concluded on Sunday evening, Ellen thanked everyone for their loving support. With her face glowing, she announced that she had decided she wanted to live. There wasn't a dry eye in the room as everyone expressed their happiness at her embracing of life. Three months later, she phoned to tell us that her doctor was shocked to discover that her cancer had gone into full remission. She remains cancer free six years later.

Hatred for the physical reveals itself in many other ways. Feeling burdened, helpless, and powerless over the circumstances of their life, people may console themselves with a belief or hope that salvation will come after death. In our therapy work, we often hear clients express a romanticized notion of death and the hereafter, usually accompanied by a large dollop of self-pity due to their plight in life.

Oscar

This life-negating perspective is sometimes a result of unresolved childhood issues or trauma. A client named Oscar lost his mother when he was five years old. As is often the case with children, Oscar had internalized the feeling that somehow he was to blame for this tragedy. He carried this pain into adulthood, and the shame and guilt he felt for not being able to save his mother pervaded his life.

During a weekend workshop, Oscar explained to the group how important a role spirituality and meditation played in his life. He said that more than anything, he longed for the afterlife, so that he would, as he put it, "no longer be confined by the restraints of the physical world."

However, later in the weekend, he was telling the group that he wanted to find his soulmate. At that point, I had to stop him and asked, "How are you going to have a committed relationship when you seem to have an even stronger commitment to leaving this world?" This stunned him into a thoughtful silence until he said, "You're right; I never thought about that." We helped Oscar look more deeply into his longing for the afterlife, and what came to the surface was his unresolved relationship with his mother and an unconscious desire to be reunited with her in death.

In working with many clients, we have also noticed that the longing for the beyond sometimes comes up at a critical juncture in the therapeutic process. When a particularly painful layer of the onion comes to the surface of their awareness, they feel it's just too much to face and they'd rather bail out, wishing they could just die instead. In Oscar's case, he had sublimated his wish to die into a comforting spiritual belief that kept the painful truth at bay.

Barbara

Barbara was a woman in her late forties who came to us feeling depressed and understandably upset about serious menstrual bleeding that went on well past the normal duration of her period. Her doctors were unable to determine the physiological source of her problem. During a private session, it came to the surface that she always felt inadequate in her female body, in part because her father had often expressed disappointment at not having a son; that she was after all, "just a daughter." Barbara carried feelings of helplessness and hopelessness about being in a female body, believing she could never be as powerful as a man. Every time she had a period, and later, when she entered menopause, she felt victimized and held back by her female nature. Her uterus had literally been crying out for help. We often see physical metaphors like this that are acting out the problem and need to be heeded. We helped her release all the emotional and physical manifestations of her hatred for the female body. Her excessive bleeding stopped the next day, and she resumed having healthy and regular periods.

There are many shared similarities amongst those who have hatred for the physical. Some of these patterns are addressed in the following e-mail that I sent to a client:

For many of us, the shock of coming into the physical body is overwhelming because of our longing for whence we came. We forget that we willingly signed up for this incarnation. In this forgetfulness, we may numb ourselves with cigarettes, alcohol, and comfort food, not wanting to be fully present and conscious.

As to answer your question about why you are still here; Besides the aspect of you that has disdain for being here in the physical, there is another aspect that made a sacred contract with your soul to come into the physical and learn certain lessons. These lessons are needed so that you can accomplish your soul purpose and mission here on Earth. But you continue to run from your purpose. Much of the discomfort you've been experiencing comes from the conflict between these two aspects: the one that wants to run from it all versus the one that wants to be awake and see the bigger picture and honor what you came here to do.

Also, when you feel overwhelmed by the pain of your life, you move into resignation, forgetting that there is a purpose beyond the pain. I also see the part of you who's convinced she has to keep the boxing gloves on to survive. After so many rounds of putting up a good fight, she thinks she deserves a good drink, a dessert, or a joint as a reward. And the cycle repeats. I hope this helps. Perhaps reading it in black and white will help it penetrate and stay with you.

Of course it is tough and challenging to wind our way through this Earthly realm of disease, pain, loss, and the aging process. But we must remain mindful of the fact that no matter how consciously or unconsciously we were conceived, we chose this incarnation. We must honor this choice and be open to the many lessons being provided through our life experiences. We are either actively moving toward or celebrating our purpose in being here or else stubbornly insisting that this beautiful planet is actually a waiting room of suffering until we die.

This view of the world as a realm of pain from which we pray to be delivered is drummed into us from an early age, particularly those of us raised Christian. Take for example the following passage from a Catholic prayer: "...poor banished children of Eve, to thee do we lift up our sighs, mourning, and weeping in this valley of tears."

How different, for example, is the view of the world as seen by the North American Indian. The Indians have historically always seen the physical world as their mother and have known that by living in harmony with nature, they are already in Paradise. Why long for the hereafter when, if we take the challenge of it and embrace the physical, we can become fulfilled and even enlightened in the here and now?

EXERCISE
Uncovering Your Yes and No to Life

There are times when it is obvious to us that we are saying yes to life and times when it is clear that we are saying no.

For example, Louise said no to life each time she took a drink. However, someone else may have a drink as a function of their yes. In other words, we are asking you to look at your motivation. It is not *what* you do, it's *how* you do it.

Reflect on your lifestyle and, using the chart below, write down the different ways you notice you say no to life. Then in the next column, remembering that we are at choice in each moment, write how your no can be changed into yes.

List the ways you say no to life.	How can you change your no into yes?

RELEASING PROCESS

- I release all reluctance and resentment for having to be in a physical body.

- I release my shock from when I came into the physical body and felt overwhelmed by the density here.

- I release the decision I made that being in the physical body keeps me separate from God. The truth is that the presence of God is, and always has been, anchored deep in my heart.

- I release my longing to rejoin loved ones who have died before me.

- I release the effects of thinking and believing that where those loved ones have gone is a far better place then this.

- I release my hate for being in a physical body while my loved ones were allowed to leave.

- I ask the God within me to reconnect me now to that part of my Spirit that broke off to go and be with my departed loved ones.

- I release avoiding and postponing my mission here on Earth.

- I release my belief and conviction that we live in a "valley of tears."

- I make a new decision to open up to my purpose, to love, and to a celebration of my life.

- I release my fear of being alive.

- I release my fear that I don't have a place on this Earth that is really mine.

- I release my fear that I won't live up to the expectations of others.

- I release my fear that I will never find the love in my life I so desperately am seeking.

16

Hindrance #9:
Inability to Trust Existence

The seed cannot know what is going to happen, the seed has never known the flower. And the seed cannot even believe that it has the potentiality to become a beautiful flower. Long is the journey, and it is always safer not to go on that journey because unknown is the path; nothing is guaranteed. Nothing can be guaranteed. Thousand and one are the hazards of the journey, many are the pitfalls—and the seed is secure, hidden inside a hard core. But the seed tries, it makes an effort; it drops the hard shell which is its security, it starts moving. Immediately the fight starts; the struggle with soil, with the stones, with the rocks. And the seed was very hard and the sprout will be very, very soft and dangers will be many.

There was no danger for the seed, the seed could have survived for millennia, but for the sprout many are the dangers. But the sprout starts toward the unknown, toward the sun, toward the source of light, not knowing where, not knowing why. Great is the cross to be carried, but a dream possesses the seed and the seed moves.

The same is the path for man. It is arduous. Much trust and courage will be needed.

—Osho, *Osho Zen Tarot Deck*

Many of us struggle with that delicate balance between being in charge of our lives and surrendering, letting go, knowing that Existence is in fact supporting us in each moment. This challenge is illustrated in my favorite Osho story as told by one of his disciples, Ma Dharma Jyoti, in her book *One Thousand Tales for One Thousand Buddhas*. It is a wonderful reminder of this delicate balance.

> *The train is about to leave, yet His luggage has not yet arrived: it was put in another car. We become worried. He is leaving to conduct a meditation camp, and I start wondering how he can manage there without his clothes. Suddenly He turns back and looks at me. I feel ashamed to disturb Him with my doubting mind—He just smiles at me. His trusting, shining eyes are still floating in the air before me as I write. I relax and remember His words, "Trust Existence."*
>
> *The guard blows the whistle again, and Osho gets in the train without His luggage. He stands at the door and looks at everyone with His mischievous smile. Somewhere in my heart I know that the train will not leave till his luggage arrives. We are all waiting there, holding our breath, to see what happens next. How unconsciously we are behaving in the presence of our enlightened master. But His compassion is infinite: He has accepted us as we are and never gives us the feeling of being ignorant or unconscious.*
>
> *Very slowly the train starts, and to our great surprise we see Ishwabhai's driver come running with His suitcase, pushing everyone aside, he reaches His compartment, and places the suitcase behind Osho, who is still standing at the door to say one more time, "Good-bye" to us.*

Years ago, when I read that passage, I wept, because this simple story, told with the love of a surrendered disciple, showed me how much mistrust still lived inside of me. Seeing Existence as the metaphorical Master, I became aware of my lack of surrender. I saw how after many lifetimes, and because of my early childhood conditioning, the common memory of my oneness with Existence was corrupted, damaging my ability and willingness to trust fully in Existence. Seeing the delayed luggage also as a metaphor, I could imagine the moments in my life when the luggage was supposed to be there and how often in my life I carried the expectation that the luggage would never arrive. And yet it has always arrived.

I was also reminded of my summers during college when I assisted at a camp for the disabled. We would often work with the campers, exercising them in the pool. Some of them were paraplegics, and I remember how difficult it was for some of them to be immersed in the water. The fear that they would sink like a stone if they dared to trust the swimming instructor was almost palpable. I remember one little ten-year-old boy in particular whose body would immediately tense as I gently lowered him into the water. Even though it was very warm, and I constantly reassured him that I was there, he would tighten up and sink. Other children developed the knack to relax their bodies, trust, and float. A serene smile would spread across their faces. I was now faced with all the ways I tensed up in life, unwilling to trust that the waters of Existence would support me in floating.

I began to see how my unwillingness to heed my Master's words to trust Existence was keeping me in a tense and doubting state of being. Like so many people, I had an addiction to knowing the how and why in my life and future. I was determined to heal this and turn it around, but how?

Hugh and I were always inspired by the Lindwalls, who taught us the Releasing work, and by how they lived their lives. Using a form of kinesiology, or muscle-testing, they always checked in with Spirit to determine what course of action was in their highest good to follow. This method guided every one of their trips to more then thirty countries to teach and share The Releasing Process.

Hugh and I would flirt with muscle testing on occasion, but at a certain point, we sensed it was time for us to up the ante if in fact we were sincere in our desire to increasingly trust Existence and operate in a world where it was trust that informed us rather than an accumulation of doubts and fears from prior lifetimes.

We decided to conduct an experiment of trust when our lives were shaken by something unexpected. We'd been living in Tiburon, California, in a home we loved. It was a three-bedroom condo with a huge deck that overlooked the San Francisco Bay and Mt. Tamalpais. It included a large office that could fit fifteen people comfortably for small workshops. We had a heated pool where I swam my mile everyday. Our neighbors were nice and the rent was very reasonable. Then, just before Christmas, our landlord told us he was raising the rent five hundred dollars per month. We were shocked! This also provoked fears and irrational beliefs that had been lurking under the surface of our consciousness. We felt victimized by our landlord, by the economy, and even by Existence. It rekindled the fear that this would constantly happen to us as long as we were renters. Feelings of hopelessness arose as we convinced ourselves that we could never afford to own our own home in Marin County, where real estate seemed only to be for the affluent.

Wading through this initial phase of despondency, we reminded ourselves that just two weeks earlier, we had decided to up the ante in the Trust Department. Now here was Existence giving us a perfect opportunity. It was a chance to test an old saying, "In the winter some people freeze and some people ski."

Using our muscle-testing technique, we began going through the classified ads, asking Spirit's help in finding our new divine home. We were surprised when we received guidance to rent a one-bedroom condominium in a little East Bay hamlet called Point Richmond. The complex was fairly new and it had a pool for me to do my laps, but the rooms were small and the walls were paper thin.

Yet every time we checked in with Spirit, we got a clear, affirmative response to move there. Dragging our feet, we moved into our new home. I think I cried every day the first month we lived there. Half of our stuff was in storage, and we were miserable in this little hobbit hole. The only saving grace was that we were allowed to sign a lease for just six months.

As it turned out, that six months became a twenty-four-hour-a day Releasing Intensive for the both of us. Living in such close quarters brought so much of our garbage to the surface that it felt almost unbearable at times. It seems that Spirit had taken us out of the sleepiness of our comfort zone and demanded that we face all those places in our lives where we were not walking our talk. As the anger, blame, mistrust, and fears came up, we used them as grist for the mill of our healing process, releasing the negative patterns and feelings day after day. Hugh and I were committed to looking at those places that had become corrupted inside us. Together we went back into the old memories and released the effects that still dominated our lives in any way.

After our six-month lease finally expired, we felt it was time for a reprieve. We scoured the classifieds, using the muscle-testing technique, and got a strong yes to check out a place in northern Marin. I had always said I would never live that far north, and when we saw the unattractive facade of this townhouse we almost drove away. But we reminded ourselves of the yes of guidance and knocked on the door. As the landlady walked us through, we were delighted to see it had everything we wanted in a home. We even whispered to each other, "I'd love to own this place someday." To make a long story short, we moved in, and in two short years, through some very magical and creative financing, we were able to buy the house that made our hearts sing. Through the wisdom of hindsight, we saw how Spirit helped us move heaven and Earth, not to mention our mistrusting egos, so we could own our divine home.

Trusting Existence is an ongoing, challenging process, especially when you are addicted to running the show, thinking and believing that you know what's best for yourself. All of my knowingness and being in charge could not have created the outcome that our six months in Point Richmond ended up giving us. The spiritual ego may even convince us that we can know what to expect when we're trusting Existence—perhaps some notion of contentedness and calm. In fact, the experience may be entirely uncomfortable, confusing, and chaotic. It is only in retrospect that we can we see the symmetry and exquisite timing of it all.

There comes a time when we just have to throw up our hands and say to Spirit, "Okay I, can't do it alone anymore; I need your help." When Hugh was a little boy in the fifties, his mother struggled with depression. Over a period of ten years, she was in and out of institutions, where she was given over a hundred shock treatments, psychotherapy, and stupefying medication. Nothing helped. One day, she was reading the Bible and came to the words, "Thy will, not my will be done." She reflected on that phrase and finally said to God, "If it is Your will that I remain hospitalized for the rest of my life and not be with my family anymore…all right then, I give up." A few weeks later, she was able to return home. Her depression lifted and never returned.

A distinction must be made here between acceptance and resignation. Resignation has a quality of the submissive victim, almost a bitterness. However, with acceptance, there is serenity and willingness to totally let go.

We all have experiences of feeling like our nose is being pressed up against a brick wall. We wonder what possible value or meaning there can be during such an awful time. We are overwhelmed by the negative feelings and gory details. Although it's difficult, this is the time we must look inward to see what needs to be released. Slowly, we will return to that state of remembrance and a visceral knowingness that Existence really *is* providing what we need—though it may take weeks, months, or even years to fully assimilate and appreciate the lesson.

Finally, we see that our luggage, even if it seems "late," has always arrived precisely at the right time.

EXERCISES
Uncovering Your Trust and Mistrust

1. List five areas in your life in which you have found it difficult to trust Existence:
    1.
    2.
    3.
    4.
    5.

2. List five areas in which you have found it easy to trust Existence:
    1.
    2.
    3.
    4.
    5.

Trusting Existence is a process of seeing all those places where your trust became corrupted and your ego, who wants to soldier through, took over.

- Close your eyes for a minute and ask Spirit Most High to take you back in time to the point of origin when your trust in Existence was corrupted.

- Ask Spirit to take you forward in time from that place and heal every incident that got placed on top of that and has kept you in a place of mistrust. Stay with each experience until it feels neutralized.

The following Releasing statements can assist you arriving at neutrality.

RELEASING PROCESS

- I release my belief that I am not the kind of person who receives guidance.

- I release my belief that other people get guidance and I don't.

- I release my fear of my future.

- I release allowing the dark side to block me understanding this.

- I release from my spleen the fear that it has carried all these years that I can't trust my future.

- I release the effects of feeling I was raised without a safety net.

- I release my belief that I still can't trust my future.

- I release my belief that if I don't secure my future all by myself, I will never be safe.

- I release my overresponsibility in making it happen all by myself.

- I release my feeling that to trust Existence would be too big a leap for me.

- I release all the hate I've stored in my thymus gland from fearing my future.

- I release from my thymus the fear that I am in imminent danger.

- I release from my spleen and third chakra the belief that I can't trust my future.

- I release the inherited fear from my mother and her mother and her mother of the future and my safety in that future.

- I release the inherited fear, worry and concern from my mother and the fear that entered me directly from my mother that she could not provide a safe future for me.

- I release the pain in my spleen from worrying about the safety and security and assuredness of my future.

- I release the effects of living with this fear for so long that I think it's normal and don't even feel it.

- I release my belief that no matter how much I surrender to Spirit, and no matter how much I ask Spirit to take care of me, Spirit will not guarantee or assure my future.

- I'm sorry, Spirit, for not trusting you.

- I release my expectation that something will go awfully wrong in my future and there won't be a safety net to sustain me.

- I release the layers of sadness from not being able to trust that my future is secure.

- I make a new decision; My future is secure.

- I release daring Spirit to prove the truth of this to me as soon as it comes out of my mouth. The truth is that no matter what I think and feel, Spirit is always with me. I choose to anchor this presence in my heart and allow it now to fill every one of my cells.

17

Hindrance #10:
Unwillingness to Serve

Not everyone can be famous, but everyone can be great,
because greatness is determined by service.

—Martin Luther King

As we have stressed throughout this book, to have a successful and fulfilling life, in the truest sense of those words, your heart must be open and engaged. The uniqueness of your particular gifts and the way you offer those gifts is determined by the degree to which you are available through your heart. You demonstrate a healthy heart when you show a willingness to serve. And conversely, an unwillingness to serve is an indication that there are ways that your heart is still closed and in need of healing.

But what is service? The word implies an enormous spectrum of possibilities, ranging from being a cocktail waitress to devoting your life to work in an orphanage in Calcutta.

What we are referring to is a quality of giving from the heart to another with no hidden agenda or expectation of something in return.

The specifics of the service and the degree of involvement is secondary; first and foremost is this quality that resides in the heart. When this quality is present, we are opening ourselves to the reciprocal flow and harmony of the universe that carries with it a generosity of spirit, abundance, and compassion.

Genuine service comes from a full and grateful heart, from an overflowing of our own cup. However, there is a danger—and it is a common pitfall—to try to be of service when one's cup is still empty. This type of generosity and service is idealistic and imitative. It's based on a belief that we *should* be of service or includes a subtle expectation of getting something in return.

Even if you have the best of intentions, if you try to serve when your inner experience is still one of neediness, you will either give yourself away, burn out, or set up unhealthy, codependent relationships. The classic, although extreme, example of this is the spouse of the alcoholic trying to "help" and "protect" him (or her) through lies, denial, and avoidance of conflict.

It's important to question your own motives for even seemingly innocent attempts at service or "helping." Many of us are so out of touch with ourselves that we easily lose a sense of what is an appropriate action in a situation. We can be so intent on caring for others or pleasing them or pacifying them or avoiding conflict that we don't clearly face our own needs.

Because of religious conditioning and childhood experiences, you may have been made to feel guilty about taking care of yourself emotionally. The fact is, your foremost responsibility is to *be selfish* for as long as it takes to heal your own wounds, develop your inner self, and fill your own cup.

It's essential to develop a strong sense of your own worth and self-respect before even thinking about service. True generosity and healthy service evolve naturally as your heart heals and opens. In this way, you also develop healthy boundaries and an ability to say no. You sense when it's time to retreat and recharge your own battery, or when it's clear that reaching out to serve another is not being helpful. It is not always the best thing to reach out and be helpful. The Buddha was usually of great service, but this was not always the case, as this story shows:

Once a powerful disagreement broke out amongst his monks in one of his forest monasteries. When Buddha arrived he recommended that they all apologize to one another, but his own monks ignored his advice. He tried a number of ways to get them to listen to him and finally realized there was nothing to do but leave them to their own consequences. So he left the unruly monks and spent a peaceful rainy season in the forest, living with the animals around him. He did what he could and no more.

The discernment of when to serve requires the use of your intuition and a constant checking in at each moment. Sometimes, giving a homeless person a dollar may be in the highest good for the both of you, and sometimes it's not. To rely on a hard and fast rule to always give or never give is a way of avoiding an opportunity to tune in each time. Every moment is unique.

When I was in my late twenties, I became a sannyasin (disciple) of the enlightened Master Osho. It was a very growthful time as I threw myself into all the different therapy groups that were available. I was impressed by the therapists' knack for facilitating inner shifts for people that resulted in major breakthroughs in their outer lives. These therapists' intuitive abilities and commitment to serving others with compassion and detachment inspired me. I remember during one of these groups thinking, This is what I want to do. But when I hung my shingle out at the ripe old age of twenty-nine and advertised my groups, clients weren't exactly lining up outside the door. After months of frustration, I wrote to Osho for some advice.

Weeks later, when I received his response, I wept at his loving suggestion: To fill my own cup first. There was also a gentle reminder regarding the need for meditation: "The more you empty, the more full you become." I did not yet have the self-love and compassion for myself that I saw reflected back in the eyes of many of the therapists I worked with during those years. I realized that the best way I could be of service was to make my own life work!

After several years of inner work, moving toward my own wholeness, self-love, and empowerment, I knew I was ready to serve others. The initial workshops came together with very little effort and continued to grow. Hugh and I had been together for a few years, and our love for each other had made our cups very full. It was time to share our gifts in partnership. Through our intuition, it was suggested by Spirit that we offer a workshop about money, an eight-week process that would be free of charge. We had made a commitment to follow the guidance of Spirit, so we took a deep breath and jumped in, having no idea what the lessons for us would be. It was an improvised affair, with us asking for guidance each week about what we were to do.

Interestingly, after that free workshop our income doubled, and then tripled.

We hadn't given the workshop as a strategy to make more money. It came out of the love in our hearts for this work and our commitment to serve humanity and Spirit. The point is, if you are feeling lethargic and uninspired, then offering something that you love to do out of service is a good way of kick-starting your energy, no matter what your field of endeavor.

Regularly tuning in to your inner guidance for suggestions on how to best provide service is also highly recommended. This can be done in conjunction with meditation, Releasing, or simply by asking Spirit to send you an indicator, a sign, to tell you how best to express yourself through service. Recently, Spirit guided us to offer a place in one of our workshops free of charge to a friend of a friend. We hardly knew her, and yet Spirit kept giving us this woman's name with the message to phone and make the offer. When we talked, she thanked me profusely, saying that she was looking for some direction in her life, and the workshop felt like the perfect thing for her to do.

We understand that this can seem like quite a challenge, especially if you are in survival mode, believing that you can't afford the time or money to extend yourself any further. Even if you have filled your own cup, your first chakra (the survival center, located at the base of the spine) may still be clamoring that you don't have enough to share, or your mind may insist that people will take advantage of you. Often, these are simply old tapes and programs continuing to inform you of your limitations. When we succumb to these fears and thought forms, the question that we dwell on is more likely, "What am I going to get?" instead of, "What can I give; how can I serve?"

The following case studies illustrate two divergent ways of missing out on the potential gifts inherent in healthy service. In the first case, the person has extended herself too far; in the second example, not far enough.

Evelyn

Here is an example of confusing service with sacrifice. Evelyn was a woman in her early forties, with no children. She'd participated in many of our workshops, but things really seemed to come to a head for her during a workshop about identifying one's purpose. We knew she had a lot on her plate in all areas of her life. She was having difficulty with her husband, as it wasn't a nurturing relationship. She was also having financial problems, partly because the work she did, in a social service capacity, paid next to nothing.

Whenever we asked Evelyn what she believed her purpose was, she always responded in a vague way, saying, "I just want to be of service to the planet." On this particular day, a Sunday, she had arrived late for the class for the third time. Apologizing, she said she'd had to pay an emergency visit to a client's home. She was tired, had a bad cold, and was stressed out. She went into a long explanation of how this house call had been a part of her service. When she finished, I couldn't help but say to her, "Evelyn, you've got to put your tits back in your blouse." After the resulting stunned silence in the room, Evelyn acknowledged that what I said was true and began to cry. Her service was actually sacrifice and a form of codependence that left her unfulfilled and depleted.

We spent the next hour delving into how her life had brought her to this point. It became apparent that the way she served was to carry the weight of other people's problems on her shoulders, and while she kept herself busy trying to fix others' lives, she was conveniently avoiding facing her own. An additional component to her skewed perception of service came from a spiritual ideal passed on from her mother, that to be selfless was to be spiritual.

Henry

Henry believed that service is only for do-gooders. He came to us because of problems in his marriage. His wife had given him an ultimatum that if he didn't spend less time on his job and share more of himself at home with her and the kids, it was over. He was immersed in the computer world of Silicon Valley and sometimes even slept at the office. It was a classic case of the workaholic father who convinced himself he was doing the right thing for his family by working so hard.

But in assisting Henry, we uncovered a deep-seated belief, inherited from his father, that it is the wife's responsibility to supply the warmth and affection to the children. This was not something Henry consciously believed, and he was embarrassed and ashamed when it came to the surface.

When we asked if he was willing to heal this old pattern, he was eager to take our suggestions. It was nearing Thanksgiving, and we arranged through a mutual friend for Henry to help at a church in San Francisco to set up for their yearly Thanksgiving dinner for the homeless. Henry followed through, and even brought along his twelve-year-old son.

Two weeks later, Henry enthusiastically reported back to us that the Thanksgiving experiment had been a great heart opener for him, and that he had donated eight computers to the computer training program at the church. His son also volunteered to go with his dad to train homeless parishioners how to use the computers. Henry's family life was back on track; his priorities in order.

To put the world in order, we must first put the nation in order;
to put the nation in order, we must first put the family in order;
to put the family in order, we must first cultivate our personal
life; we must first set our hearts right.

—Confucius

Do you associate service with obligation or with joy? Is it easier for you to deal with other people's problems instead of your own? Or do you tend to lean the other way and isolate yourself from your community?

Most of us have some deficiency in the area of service: We either have an overblown idea of service or underestimate the value of service in our life. It is a constant balancing act between maintaining healthy boundaries and extending ourselves too far. The following exercises and Releasing will give you a better idea of where your attention is needed in the realm of service.

EXERCISE
Buying a Gift

We encourage you to fully engage yourself in this exercise, because even though it seems rather simple, it is an excellent barometer for your heart's state of health regarding service.

Your assignment is to buy someone a gift. The cost and type of the item is entirely up to you, but you must follow some very specific criteria in order to get the most out of this exercise.

- The item or expense is not a sacrifice for you in any way.

- Do not give it because you think the recipient needs it.

- Do not perceive the person as incapable of manifesting it for themselves.

- Give the gift freely, expecting nothing in return, as an expression of your love.

- Keep notes on what transpires as you begin and then take this process through to completion.

- Pay attention especially to any considerations and yeah-buts.

- This information will indicate where your energy would best be applied in creating a healthy relationship with service.

RELEASING PROCESS

(if your tendency is to offer too much "service"):

- I release the pain in my heart from when I was little and felt helpless to make my parents happy.

- I release the effects of the sadness and guilt that there was nothing I could do to help them.

- I release the layers of helplessness and feeling powerless I took on as a child.

- I release the effects of feeling overwhelmed by those feelings of powerlessness.

- I release my reluctance to feel those feelings.

- I release the decision I made to instead save others whom I thought needed saving so I would not feel helpless.

- I release the fear of facing my own feelings and problems.

- I release my religious programming that tells me that others must always come before me.

RELEASING PROCESS

(if you aren't offering any service to your community):

- I release the bands of steel from around my heart that have been protecting me all these years.

- I release my fear that others will reject my love (and my service).

- I release all the programming that separates me from my humanity, telling me to only look out for Number One.

- I ask the God within to daily show me all the ways I can be of service.

CONCLUSION

Having read through and worked with The Ten Hindrances to Your Heart's Desires, no doubt you have recognized some of the ways you are playing it small, not yet fully embracing and exploring all that life is offering you.

We remind you to refer back to the blueprint that you filled out, so you can see which of the hindrances still prevent you from turning your blueprint into reality.

If you truly allow yourself to acknowledge and see all the ways you are limiting yourself, then feelings of sadness, anger, and even despair will want to come to the surface. We cannot stress enough the importance of allowing these emotions to flow. This is a healthy and natural response, and as uncomfortable as it may be, the free expression of your emotions will open you up to a deeper experience of your heart and your Being.

As you engage the energy of this deep and vulnerable space, your Releasing statements will carry much weight and potency. Instead of being a mere intellectual exercise, The Releasing Process will be a powerful vehicle in bringing healing, transformation, and divine guidance into your life.

EPILOGUE

The Releasing Process works like a bow and arrow.

Even though the target is in front of you, an arrow must be pulled in the opposite direction to gain the power it needs to fly toward the target. Similarly, with the Releasing work, it's necessary to go inside ourselves and revisit the old demons that continue to hold sway over our life. By exposing those demons to the light of day, we can reclaim our power and then move forward, embracing a life informed by inner peace and outer success.

In our culture, most adults have a huge amount of energy tied up in their old programs and fears from the past. As inner-child therapist John Bradshaw has said, "The estimated percentage of dysfunctional families in western culture is seventy percent. As I've delved more deeply into counseling, I believe it's more likely to be one hundred percent!" Only by returning to those unsettling memories and childhood decisions that still control us can we truly set ourselves free, utilizing all the energy that was tied up in the past to fuel and empower us in the present.

Of course, we all have a chorus of inner voices that discourage such a quest. The ego fights this process tooth and nail because it wants to avoid anything that is painful or even remotely threatening to its existence. The intellect points out how illogical it is to focus one's attention on anything but strategies for survival in the chess game of life. The mind with all its knowledge and accomplishments insists that it is very comfortable and satisfied with what it already has, but it secretly fears losing control, being made wrong, and ultimately, humbled.

But our inner Being, with its hunger for truth and liberation, is our champion. If we will only listen to its still small voice emanating from our heart, it will give us the courage we need to overrule those other voices and bravely step into the holy fire of self-inquiry.

As with the drawing back and then releasing of the bowstring, the inner work of releasing negative feelings and limiting beliefs unleashes a tremendous amount of energy to propel you forward. Very often, clients are depressed and lethargic when they first come to see us, but after a Releasing session, they are delighted and amazed at the newfound energy and enthusiasm they feel. If they continue with their healing process, more and more they experience feeling like a full cup instead of an empty one. When our cup is empty, life remains in a holding pattern of merely surviving, often with numerous physical ailments that drain our resources even further. Only when our cup is full do we have the vitality, stamina, and compassion to drink life fully, relate in a healthy way to others, and offer our gifts and service to the world.

It appears that the therapeutic work of Releasing is personal and private, but paradoxically, in a very real way, it connects us to our heritage and to all of humanity. We carry not only our own pain but also that of our parents, grandparents, and past generations. As Jung has written, through the collective unconscious, we each carry all of the experiences of humanity, glimpses of which we often see in our dreams. So as we reach deeply inside ourselves to feel and release our own psychic pain, we are fulfilling an invaluable service of releasing collective pain for the human race.

Committing to one's inner healing journey contributes to nothing less than the evolution of the human race toward a more harmonious and loving future. It is our wish and prayer that you, our readers will summon the courage required to accept this challenge.

May your arrow fly straight, loving, and true.

ABOUT THE AUTHORS

For over eighteen years Voge and Hugh Smith have brought a contagious joy to their workshops and private sessions. Combining their separate and unique talents they have an inspiring partnership that promotes trust and a true listening for all participants. Voge and Hugh have facilitated profound healing and change for thousands of clients, helping them achieve new milestones of success in their personal and professional lives.

Voge is a gifted clairvoyant and was trained in The Releasing Process by the Lindwalls in 1990. She serves on the Board of the Lindwall Foundation and has a private counseling practice in the San Francisco Bay Area.

After a career in education, Hugh managed the Osho Arvind Meditation Center in Vancouver, Canada, before moving to the States.

Toward Wholeness Seminars evolved out of their marriage and their commitment to support individuals in living the life that makes their heart sing!

Eleven years ago, they created *The Metaphor Course* which combines powerful and effective experiential exercises with The Releasing Process. During the course Voge and Hugh offer a pragmatic spirituality that guides participants into an understanding of the deeper lessons underlying troubling life issues, be it with money, health, relationship or spirituality. Hence these problems are seen as Metaphors rather than crippling obstacles.

The Metaphor Course is offered several times a year in Novato, CA.
If you would like to bring *The Metaphor Course* to your community, please contact Voge and Hugh through their website at www.towardwholeness.com or call 415.382-8162

To find out more about Voge and Hugh Smith

and the courses they offer through
Toward Wholeness Seminars, contact them at:

www.towardwholeness.com
info@towardwholeness.com
415.382.8162

To order additional copies of *I Release!* or the Releasing CDs, fill out the form below and mail to:

Toward Wholeness Seminars
900 Bel Marin Keys Blvd.
Novato, CA 94949
Make checks payable to Voge & Hugh Smith. Please allow three weeks for delivery.
Sorry, we cannot accept credit cards at this time.

Order Form
Please photocopy this form if additional copies are needed.

Books	Price	Quantity	Total
I Release!	15.95		
CD			
Spiritual Fitness through the Chakras	20.00		
Releasing the Hindrances to Your Heart's Desires	15.00		
		Shipping: $3.00 *	

Total: _____

* Kindly contact us for shipping prices on bulk orders.

Ship to:

_____ Name

_____ Address 1

_____ Address 2

_____ Daytime phone

_____ E-mail address

144

NOTES

0-595-31290-X